Dear Reader:

We appreciate your purchase and use of our materials, and pray God's richest blessing of enlightenment and education upon your enjoyment of your new text. As this work is a combination teaching and study guide, it is understood that your new book will be used for your personal study and development.

The comprehensive nature of this publication, however, means this text includes lessons, planning guides, lecture outlines, assignments and casework, practicum, and reviews. Collectively, these comprise the elements of a curriculum and are the reasons this and many of our other our texts frequently find themselves in group studies, classrooms, schools, seminars, and workshops. To assure proper regard is given the author for the material, the publisher gives no permission for any reader or user to reproduce, resale, or distribute this book in whole or in part without written authorization. Should the intended use of this work be as a supplement or complement to an existing curriculum or as a lone course, written permission from the publisher is also necessary before distributing and/or teaching students.

Whenever the subject matter contained in this book is taught or referred to publicly, proper recognition and acknowledgment of its author and title are required to assure due credit for the work is given to its originator. The same applies to minuscule excerpts taken from the book for use in other writings, in which a written release for such use must be secured from the publisher first.

Thank you,

Dr. Paula A. Price
Author

Flaming Vision Publications
Tulsa, OK

The Five-Fold Offices

Paula A. Price, D. Min., PhD

Flaming Vision Publications
Tulsa, Oklahoma

The Five-Fold Offices
Unless otherwise indicated, all scripture quotations are from the King James Version of the Bible.
© 1994 by Everlasting Life Ministries, Inc., P.O. Box 5686, Hillside, NJ 07205
Printed in the United States of America.
ISBN 1-886288-13-5 Library of Congress, Pending

TABLE OF CONTENTS

Introduction

CHRIST

The Church

Ground

Apostle		Prophet

Pillar

Apostles	Prophets	Teachers
Operations		
Miracles • Healings • Helps • Tongues • Interpretations		
(Gifts)		

Prophecy	Faith
Ministry	Teaching
Exhortation	Liberality
Leadership	Mercy
Stewardship	Oration
Revelation	Activities

The Five-Fold

About the Five-Fold Offices

A Quick Review

No significant study of the Five-fold Offices would be complete without an appreciation of its foundations. The foundation disclosed in Ephesians 4, where Paul unveils far the Church, the positions installed by Christ at his ascension to serve his church as long as it remains on earth. In preparation, therefore, for what we are to cover, we will spend a few moments reviewing them.

The five-fold ministry offices outlined in Ephesians 4:11 are the appointed positions Christ installed in his Body upon his ascension. Having given his disciples the charges of Matthew 28:18-20, Luke 24:44-49 and Mark 15:15-20, he provided them an organized structure within which to carry out his Program. The five-fold ministry offices exist for the express purpose of carrying out for Christ the Mission His Father entrusted to Him, through the work of the church on earth. The following may be thought of as the Eleven Descriptives of Christian Ministry:

- Preach the Gospel

- Make Disciples

- Baptize Disciples

- Teach Disciples

- Heal the Sick

- Motivate salvation's repentance

- Inspire Disciple Sanctification

- Qualify Disciples to Receive Inheritance

- Equip Disciples for Ministry

- Train Disciples for Ministry

- Prepare Disciples for Eternal Life

The Ministry Is Christ's

It should be pointed out here that the ministry, all of the offices and operations, etc., is born Christ's. His Father gave the mission and the subsequent ministries to him upon his ascension. As Ephesians 4:7-8 will tell you, He in turn gave gifts to men, as foretold in Psalm 68. Christ gave to those who entered his kingdom gifts of services, allowing them to take part in his mission and his work. It is erroneous to claim personal prerogatives over the ministries the Lord has given us. We are but helpers to Him in his effort to restore us to life and redeem us back to his Father God.

What the Ministry Consists Of

The ministry consists of diverse gifts, different ministries, different activities or operations— *All to manifest the living God by the Holy Spirit.*

When he dispenses the Grace needed for our services and its different privileges, honors and authority; along with powers needed to get our assigned jobs done, it is according to both the counsel of His will and His creator foreknowledge of us. The Lord's dispensations are based on who we are, how we are made, and what we were made (and saved) to do. Nevertheless, the power, as Paul and the other Church Founders discovered, is God's not ours.It is for his glory, not for our personal self-inflation. The fact that we enjoy glory, too, is an attestation to the greatness of God. It signifies that there is never any mediocrity or impotence in Him; therefore, His tiniest strength turns out potency for us. That potency undoubtedly reverberates with honor, glory and awe toward us as we go about His business and services in the earth.

About The Eleven Descriptives

These descriptions represent the aims of Christ's program as handed down by the Father God. Anyone seeking to serve in them should become intimately familiar with every aim to effectively do their part in bringing them to pass on Christ's behalf.

If studied carefully one would see they disclose Christ's ministries' work and reflect their responsibilities as the ambassadors He ordains to help Him. It is this work we are going to concentrate on as we go through our study of the Prophet's Ministry. In the process, you will learn the purpose of these positions and come to understand the "big picture" God has in mind for these offices. You'll see how they are the *vital instruments* of his vision. To God they are instruments, "But to mankind they are gifts."

Afterward, we'll go over some of the important details of the office. Things like personality, functions, and natives of the officers, which will be discussed at length, as well as an explanation of leadership as it relates to the prophet. A look at the prophet's power and authority is also included. Following, the prophet's ministry itself is examined, and a section on miracles and the Occult rounds out the teaching. Each Unit contains exercises to allow you to apply your new knowledge and to reinforce your learning.

God, according to our Ephesians and Corinthians Scriptures, ordained that His churches (those established and shepherded by his Son Jesus Christ under the hand of the Holy Spirit) be staffed with nothing less than Apostles, Prophets and Teachers. He further ordained they be endued with supernatural powers and efficacy endowments to facilitate the office's mission and strengthen those who fill them in the church as long as it remains on the earth. As long as sin, Satan, man and God all remain the same—sin in man, man in darkness, and God immutable—the need for these ordinations will continue. The Church, the body of Christ at large, is to be protected by these supernatural dispensations throughout the body worldwide. Its officers busily handle the spiritual officiates intrinsic to Christ's Bride. Following are examples:

- Evangelizing and discipling the world
- Continuance of the truth
- Growth, sanctification and holiness
- Maintenance of supernatural strength
- Preservation of purity, wholeness, soundness, and overall well being
- Equipping for service
- Preparation for ministry duty
- Maturation for eternal existence
- Increasing the flock in the knowledge of God
- Stability of the faith
- Knowledgeable interaction and communion with the Godhead
-

All fall under this umbrella of the Five-fold Officer's work in the broadest possible sense.

23 Reasons for the Five-Fold

✓ Preach Gospel

✓ Make Disciples

✓ Baptize Disciples

✓ Teach Disciples

✓ Heal Sick

✓ Deliver Captives

✓ Motivate Repentance

✓ Inspire Sanctification

✓ Qualify Heirs for Blessings

✓ Equip for Service

✓ Train for Ministry

✓ Appoint Ministers

✓ Install Ministers

✓ Oversee Ministers

✓ Execute God's Will/Plan

✓ Officiate God's Affairs

✓ Impart Spiritual Gifts

✓ Perform Supernatural

✓ Promote Holiness

✓ Ready Church for Eternal Life

✓ Keep Christ the Center of the Faith

✓ Enable Fellowship with the Godhead

✓ Enable Submission to the Leadership and Government of the Holy Spirit

SPIRITUAL EQUIPMENT

For Ministry Service

Before you do anything, know and understand the following conditions for faithful, diligent service to the True & Living God! To be for him, you must possess and experience these:

Love for God

Commitment to holiness

Zeal for God's righteousness

Apprehension of divine truth

Acceptance of humanity's universal sin

Realization of sin in the flesh

Understand flock's need for maturation

Recognize need for all mankind to repent and be saved

Allegiance to God

Determination to uphold God's truth

Willingness to rebuke/warn of sin's judgment

Self-sacrifice and loss of identity

Obedience/Submission/Surrender

Proper God-approved training

Able to nurture and train the flock of God

Peculiar human insight

Strength of conviction

Defensive about the gospel

Protective of God's kingdom

Zealous safeguard of God's sheep

Hungry for God's company

Reverence for God's sovereignty

Respect for God's judgments

Little regard for the world

Contempt for worldliness

Longing for heavenly home

Aching for God's lost sheep

Certainty of final judgment

Eager to see the end of this age

Need for continuous fellowship with God

Strong sense of duty

See gravity of the office

Know scope of responsibility

Know full impact of office demands and influence

Comprehend outcome of efforts and work

These characterizations enable the serious servant to not only answer his call, but they act as the impetus he needs to succeed in his call's labors.

> *(See Manifestation, Gift Charts at end for a deeper understanding)*

KNOW YOUR WORK
AND THE VALUE OF YOUR POSITION

> ➤ EVANGELISM
> ➤ REVIVAL
> ➤ DISCIPLING

Inspiration
    Indoctrination
        Sanctification
            Organization
                Motivation
                    Preservation   *Resurrection
                        Revelation   *Glorification
                Edification
            Liberation
        Stabilization
    Application
Dedication

CHAPTER ONE
Overview and Explanations

THE FIVE-FOLD OFFICES

Overview and Explanations

In this text we will explore what has become known as The Five-fold Offices of the Church of the Lord Jesus Christ. Every effort has been made in writing it to take you from God's heart to the Church's Ministry. The ways used to analyze and compare the language chosen by God in Scripture for the offices and their functions come from their natural or earthly counterpart. Taken from positions with functions similar to what an officer does, as an agent of an organization, we have laid them against the work Christian Ministers do as officers of God's Divine organism, the Church of the Lord Jesus Christ.

The Five-Fold: Ancient Concepts Serve New Testament Function

The concept of the Five-fold Officers of Ephesians 4:11 is not new. It is not strictly a New Testament Institution. The idea of a conglomerate entity that springs of a central core (the church) branching out into distinct functions is a dated one. The Old Testament period alludes to a similar institution comprising a body of class ministers sent to perform the specialized activities of a centralized purpose. The substance of their institution resembles, broadly, the church institution described by the Apostle Paul as a single corporation of ministry; the Old Testament shadow is known as the *Melakim*. The noun is *Malak* and defines a messenger representative. The meaning includes the tasks carried out by one who is a representative. These tasks can be as simple as carrying a single message or as complex as executing a special commission. Whichever it is, the term stresses that the messenger represents his sender.

For the duration of the assignment the functionary and his sender are expeditiously one and the same. Those who serve this institution must above all have a message, as message bearing is central to the necessity of the service. This applies whether the assignment is a commission, a mission, a task, duty, function, or errand. These officers can be judges, guardians, deliverers, or protectors of God's property, His glory, possessions, and premises. They embody the presence and glory of God, ideally, and can smoothly engender His praise as part of the service. The *Melakim* could be an intercessor or a herald. He could be a teacher, a prophet, or a priest. From this statement it is clear to see how the institution foreshadowed the Church Paul was charged with organizing and establishing. It was assuredly well known to him and influenced his concept of the form and structure of the Lord's Church.

The *Melakim's* duties, depending upon his position, in addition to being a messenger, included announcing, summoning, declaring and informing. It is easy to see this as the role of the evangelist and the teacher in the church. There was prophecy, diplomacy, spying, restraining behavior, and in-gathering, along with duties of guardianship that applies to the pastor, the prophet, and the apostle. Priestly functions we accept are the entire responsibility of the church of Jesus Christ according to 1 Peter 2:19.

Not only did this institution officiate over the "religio-spiritual" matters of God's possession, but they were stewards of the nation's temporal affairs as well. They were business people, craftsmen, goods merchandiser's, skilled laborers, and professionals. You could find them performing routine tasks and projects related to the mission of spreading God's message and as professional bureaucrats. These servants were, unquestionably, God-endowed for their work regardless of its nature and were rendered productive by an unending supply of His Spirit.

No other institution researched could possibly mirror the Ephesians 4 Church better than this. No term best describes its proposed function from the mind of God than this. The titles may differ somewhat—scribes, sages, seers and rabbis—instead of those employed by Paul for the Church. Nevertheless, the concept and its express labors are clearly identified in this Old Testament Institution. Even the ministry of helps is provided for in the explanation of its works. The professional, the royal, the bureaucrat, the craftsman and merchant, the skilled laborer and the producer all have a place within the framework of the *Melakim*. Moreover, its goal is similar to the Church and is attained through the union and assignments of the Lord Jesus. Matthew 28:18-20 and Mark 16:15-20 plainly show the divinely approved work shifted, as with all the Old Testament custodies, from the natural to the spiritual; from the localized to the universal. Now the Church composed of all nations, peoples, and tongues were to see, generation to generation, to the business of proclaiming God, discipling His offspring, shepherding His flock, and of declaring His present truth. They were to attend to His affairs and regain control of His Creation from the hands and rule of darkness.

Discovering and Applying This Teaching

Several factors were considered in researching this material: purpose and function, conditions and climate, environment and consciousness, in addition to God's goal and humanity's state of existence are but a few. The approach used to present this teaching is consistent with that used by the Lord Jesus when He taught those who followed His earthly ministry. Christ stayed with the premise His Father God used throughout the record of His dealings with mankind. He based His teachings on much of what the people already understood and practiced to establish His new kingdom.

One clear way to understand the approach the Lord used is to go back and draw on the history of God's dealings with man. From the moment of Adam's fall, the Lord's methods were to be changed. Where formerly He was first and only, now another element was added to the mentality of His creation. Instead of being inclined toward God as their Creator; humanity now wrestled with a dark hostile force that stood in the way. This new force literally barricaded the path of God to man, and man's path to his God. Since God and His ways were now alien to man, the Lord was forced to retreat. Under the new era, man was to stumble through his darkness and sin to learn what was once apparent to him. He needed other ways to access his Maker to do so. For religion, worship, righteousness, etc., God would have to let the darkness precede the light and allow sin to be the ground for human righteousness: Let them get it wrong, as long as they get it, was God's initial approach to restoring His light in mankind. Later He would bring truth and the light to make it right.

Association Method of Teaching

To teach them His ways, an alternative means of teaching was required. God chose the association method of teaching. Through this method, the Lord drew on the accumulation of facts, customs, history, behaviors, and beliefs the people were already embracing. He used their language (slang included), their loves, passions—and yes, even their idols—to shatter their myths, uproot superstitions, and redirect their focus to their God. Christ taught parables using the people's major commerce, agriculture. He used employment practices, entertainment and amusements, and anything else they could relate to, to bring them from the world's darkness to God's light.

When teaching on the subject of heaven, Jesus employed an earthly replica or similitude, because the visible and earthly was what the people could readily grasp. When explaining the nature of His kingdom and installing the officers of His Church, He chose names and titles reasonably familiar to them so they would easily understand what was being transferred to the kingdom of God and how it was to be used. Psalm 78:1-3 and 29:9-14 tell why.

The basis for the Lord's method, as you can see from the Scripture references, stemmed from the natural darkness, ignorance, and opposition to God man is born with as a result of his Adamic heritage. These traits, it is accepted, were passed on through Adam's seed. While we all know the story, time and events have shown not everyone is aware of its effects.

Over the centuries, the story of man's fall and doom has been ridiculed, romanced, distorted, and even rewritten. What happened in Eden may continue to be the plot, but its consequences, the spiritual, natural, and physical side effects, have been overlooked in much the same way as guilty souls overlook or play down their faults and missteps: "It's no big deal, so why focus in on them?" is the typical attitude. However, concerning the Edenic Penalties, this dangerous position causes one to be shortsighted and thus unequipped to grasp the Compensatory Needs that arose out of, and continue to emerge from, the transgression's effect. It is these very needs that brought about the Church (a body of called-out ones) and its ministries and officers.

Compensatory Accommodations

Religious tradition has made it not only unpopular to recall the sin men fell into, but undesirable to do so as well. Prevalent church teachings have pushed the upswing outcome of the cross and severed it from the downside of the fall. Both must be *equally understood* if the institutions of God and their **compensatory accommodations** are to be ascertained and rightly addressed.

By **compensatory accommodations**, we mean the adjustments, designs, and implementations God, and men through Him, employs to make up for, overcome, and offset, the ravages of sin. Though they are essential to man, these often obstruct the Lord and stagnate His will and His redemption programs in the process. Mainly, they ease the burden of the curse.

If you were to think about all this carefully, you would acknowledge that much of what we praise as human advancement and technological explosion is just compensation for the shortfalls sin has kneaded into the nature of man. Should the Bible be taken honestly again, this truth would become evident to the astute thinker and the reasonable scholar. Here are a few cases in point. The following examples are to show you what was required to relieve the hardship of human life destroyed by sin. For instance, consider the motivation behind the inventions below:

Electricity	To remove the darkness that fell on men and the earth that brought his functional life to a grinding halt.
Refrigeration	To prolong the life of food from the natural spoilage built into it that added to man's physical sickness.
Automation	To speed up the pace of human existence; to facilitate man's travel from one place to another so he could produce.
Communication	To widen the conversation bands of verbal exchange narrowed by the

	disunity sin bred into the human makeup.
Medicine	To reverse, overturn, and stem the tide of physical suffering and maladies caused by the innate corruptions and deteriorations natural to the flesh: Sickness, disease, age, and catastrophes.
Science	To overall enrich and improve, or find the answers for, the quality (and state of) human life. Man's discoveries of the mysteries of his world, once known and understood by Adam, became locked away from his inherent human intelligence. Science is the means whereby man strives to overturn his hopelessness apart from his Maker.
Cosmetics	To cover up, modify, and beautify what sin has marred, distorted or disfigured.
Perfume	To compensate for the natural human secretions that offend the senses and are harmful to the body without regular hygiene.
Alcohol	An antidote for the weak embattled and embittered human soul, its broken emotions and ruptured psyche.
Amusement	A means of momentarily escaping life's harshness by diverting the attention from the vulnerability and temporality of human life.

These are but a few. For sure you can add more to this list yourself; you get the point, however.

Over fifty percent of what this life has to offer in business, industry, education, science, and technology subsists on the very effective coup Satan pulled off in the Garden of Eden. As a result, the faculties, capacities, mentality and physique God intended man to enjoy and to use in his world became flawed. Instead of the Heavenly Age, once man fell, he found he was left to drudge through the Sin Age. Discovery after discovery helped humanity advance from the Stone Age to the present, just to reach the place where he is today. All this he was forced to do to survive as a race and to recapture, at every stage, some semblance of his former glory. His advancements are simply necessary to ease the burden of his life.

Meanwhile, God was in the background helping him, nudging him, and preserving the seed as best He could. Man's spiritual light, being completely extinguished by the fall, severed and thus alienated him from his Maker. To get the ball rolling again God instituted a series of religious programs to redirect man's worship center back to Himself and ultimately, exchange the religious rituals for restored relationship. These He did in the midst of the carnal demonic imaginations of Cain and his posterity. Their darkness meant they would feebly and futilely try to get back to God without any help from God at all.

Failed approaches to worship began with Adam after the fall. They extended through the flood until they culminated in the fulfillment of God's dream in His Son Jesus Christ. Then the passages of scriptures like John 5:22-30, Ephesians 2:1-2; 1 Corinthians 15:20-22 became no longer true. Men ceased to be alienated from God, dead in trespasses and sins, and dead in Adam because of sin. Instead, humanity was reunited in Christ. The cross made them forgiven and saved by grace. Now those who believed were made alive—quickened by the Son of God's love.

At least one third of man's being was revived by the redemptive work of the cross. What remained preserved were the other two thirds. Progressively they are restored, repaired, and revived until the whole can be regenerated and death, the last enemy, is destroyed. By now you realize God planned all this to be accomplished through the Church *(See Ephesians 1 & 2)*. Therefore, the Lord brought forward an encoded prophecy from Psalm 68:18. Here is a portion of it, but a notable one. The verse reads, "You have ascended on high; you have led captivity captive; you have received gifts among men, even among the rebellious, that the Lord God might dwell there."

Decoded in Ephesians, written approximately A.D. 60-61, verses 4:11 show Paul's revelation of the Church's leadership and hierarchy. Linking Psalms 68:18 with Ephesians 4:11, the apostle named the fundamental offices of the Church and defined their purposes. To lay the foundation for his revelation Paul draws the Old Testament prophecy forward and sets it in the heart of his New Testament unveiling.

Reminding us of the finished work of Christ, he reiterates that Christ ascended on high, led captivity captive, and gave gifts to men. Immediately Paul answers any rising questions over the ascension. Christ who descended, he asserts, has now ascended. What was Paul's purpose? To show how Christ filled all things. Afterward, Christ distributed those Psalms 68 gifts within the Church. He was free to do so because He completed what it took for Him to possess those gifts of human treasures. Now He was able to give them to His Church so that it would be established (founded, built up, and stabilized). Through these human gifts, it would be perpetually manned, managed, covered, cared for, and nurtured *throughout* its existence on earth.

Next, we will spend some time discussing the Psalm 68 gifts and their officialdom in the kingdom of God.

The Kind of Gifts Christ Gave

The word for gifts as used here is the Greek, *Doma*. It comes from the Greek *Didomi* (Psalm 68:18). The first word means, "A gift; a present." It connotes the presentation of a gift. The second term qualifies what was presented. In our instance the gift was a "bestowal." About Paul's subject, the bestowal of a ministry in all its corresponding powers is what is meant. The implication is that the gifts were officers who were set in the Church for discrete purposes. They were to integrate the fullness of *Didomi's* meaning as they brought forth, committed themselves, (and were committed), granted and were granted, received, and showed or demonstrated what they were set in place to do throughout the world through the Church.

Although the offices were gifts, that is, *bestowals and presentations,* their authority and esteem were not to be diminished or slighted nonetheless. The gift aspect came into play when the Psalmist added, almost as a postscript, *"Even the rebellious, that the Lord God might dwell there."* The rebellious in question were, of course, the converts who were once the property of Satan, formerly vessels of his habitation.

Now that the Lord had finished His Calvary work, they became His prize trophies and New Creation vessels for the holy habitation of the Godhead. Subsequently these souls, snatched out of the world for Christ, were *given* portions of His remaining mission and ministry. Through them, Christ would oversee and tend His flock. Also, He would be able to continue evangelizing, prophesying and teaching from His heavenly throne through the officials He ordained to keep His Church going. Hence, the gift application explains the meaning of Ephesians 2:8-10.

Collectively these constituted what came to be known as the Five-fold offices of the Church. As a new organization, its staff members were endowed supernaturally from the start. All they received was given freely *(See Matthew 10)*. No one went to school, but was initially approved by God instead of man. Not one of them bought, or otherwise earned their ministry. They were, as John 15 maintains, chosen beforehand by Christ. Later schooling does not "qualify" one for his or her preordained office, nor does it establish it. What school does is help the minister to do his job better; it improves the official's performance. Whether a person is capable of doing the job or not in the beginning does not affect their divine call to the ministry of Christ. Ineptitude, inexperience, or lack of knowledge will not annul God's call. They will simply, in the end, discredit the minister's effort.

On the basis of these, the word "gift" is appropriately applied. Were you to think about it carefully you would conclude this makes perfect sense in light of who God is. Anything the Lord gives humans falls under the classification of a gift. For there is nothing we as God's creatures receive from Him that could be earned. In no way could we make ourselves eligible for our ministries. We could not buy them from Him, nor do we possess enough or could ever produce or generate enough to give the Lord in exchange for His use of us. Positively, we could not hope to trade Him for it. Why, we don't even know what type of currency He would demand! Certainly our corruptible moneys would not do. So, to clarify how we receive from the Lord, He informs us that He gives and we receive. This is the context in which the dispensations God imparts are termed as "gifts".

In our explanation of the context in which the word gift is applied in Ephesians 4:11, where we contrasted it with other uses of the word, we found the term we just evaluated appears only twice. The other occasion is in Luke 11:13.

The Gift is an Officer

Now we address the reference to the *Ephesians' staff* as officers next. You have heard this ascription before and will come upon it numerous times throughout this study. No doubt it is quite unfamiliar to you who are accustomed to seeing them as ministers, servants, and no more; and this they are. All the same, though, there is much more to be learned about what God had in mind when He made these choices and applied His select titles to them. Clearly, He had a bigger picture in mind.

Truthfully, what the Lord did not have in mind, however, was exaltation of the flesh or the inflation of egos. 1 Thessalonians tells us that He further did not intend the degradation and abuse of His officers we see so common today. Other Scriptures point out that this was the farthest thing from God's mind. The current (and traditional) neglect, despite the obnoxious treatment God's servants receive merely for answering their call and obeying His voice, is typical but not ordained. On the other hand, clergy arrogance and superiority shown toward the flock was not God's aim either. In the end, those who commit such offenses (on both sides) will have to answer for it, whether they are from among the flock or peers and colleagues; God always takes up the cause of the mistreated. Even so, the esteem (not worship) God intended His minister receives is revealed in the descriptions their meanings give.

The way the term "officer" applies in Scripture, the accompanying explanations say why their simple value may be expressed in one word: respect. Title misnomers have had the effect of fueling the contempt and offenses against these ministers' people often throw at them. Our purpose is to show how the popular "equality for all doctrines" has leveled their stations to over stretch the premise that has proved damaging. The problem with this is that what people don't respect, they won't heed. Failure to heed makes the body prey to Satan and his maneuvers. The tragic result is Hebrews 13:17: the officer's ministry ceases to be profitable to those they are charged to serve. To address the misnomers, the following information was compiled and presented to correct the misconception.

The Meaning of an Officer

An officer, according to several reliable sources, is the following: (On your own time, research each term as used for a deeper understanding).

A. An Agent

B. An Executive

C. An Administrator

D. A Judge

E. A President

F. A Minister

G. A General

H. A Chair

I. A Governor

J. A Guardian

K. A Custodian

L. A Prelate

An Officer is Also:

A. A Steward

B. An Intermediary

C. A Legate

D. A Vice

E. A Consul

F. A Spokesperson

G. An Operative

H. An Intercessor

I. An Implement

J. A Messenger

Students: research from all sources what each word means, implies, calls for and exemplifies in the space provided.

Within the title definitions listed, these five servants fill 22 definite roles. Each one's duties move them collectively in and out of their role as needed for the execution of their mission and the performance of their mandate. Both mission and mandate, you should know, are the reason for their services to the Lord. Their positions, based on these, carry huge responsibilities, and give consequences for dereliction. Of all the people the Lord anoints to stand in these offices, a scarce handful know what their mantles and assignments entail. This book will surely be a benefit to these laborers if they are to "make full proof of their ministry."

The Weight of an Office

As officers, considering the spread of responsibilities they carry, the functions of the Ephesians 4:11 positions are immense. Many of them, as they go about doing their work, are so efficient they never give thought to what they tackle and perform in their service from day to day.

The office they execute is a position of trust and authority, involving a discharge of duty. In relation to the church, an officer prescribes, authorizes, standardizes, and officiates religious service.*   His is a post of authority and is supported by derived authority. As such, the position is duly sanctioned to handle the specific affairs of the authority it carries out.   Offices constitute the branches of special concern of an organization, government, or institution (a meaningful statement that helps give insight into what the Lord had in mind), and generally fall under departments. Pertaining to the church, the government is God's, the department is Christ's mission, and the institution is the Church—His body on earth. Those who handle God's branch offices' execution preside, direct, and mange the affairs of the multitudinous assembly of God.

The three departments of the Church's divine institutions are *Apostle, Prophet, and Teacher* as stated in I Corinthians 12:28.

*By religious we mean those services detailed and upheld in Scripture, the Holy Bible canonized by the Lord Jesus Christ.

46 Five-Fold Duty Officiates

Here is the gist of what *standing in an office* entails:

1.	Communication	2.	Legislation
3.	Enactment	4.	Ordainment
5.	Constitution	6.	Lawmaking
7.	Deliberation	8.	Officiation
9.	Performing Rites	10.	Anointment
11.	Confirmation	12.	Imposing Rules
13.	Regulations	14.	Representation
15.	Arbitration	16.	Mediation
17.	Intervention	18.	Negotiation
19.	Trial	20.	Judgment
21.	Government	22.	Authority
23.	Commanding	24.	Leadership
25.	Mastery	26.	Headship
27.	Directorate	28.	Coordination
29.	Management	30.	Discipline
31.	Administration	32.	Dispensation
33.	Distribution	34.	Appointment
35.	Installation	36.	Inauguration
37.	Enforcement	38.	Guarding
39.	Canon	40.	Education
41.	Development	42.	Planning
43.	Operations	44.	Decision
45.	Organization	46.	Execution

This is but a sketch of what all the respective officers do throughout their tenure in God's service. Some things, though, are constant. That means they don't vary from post to post. Others show up, however, with greater frequency and intensity in one officer over another. They make an office an office, comprising the officiations that constitute it. An analysis drafted from the meanings and applications of all these words will produce a thorough profile to enrich the Church's understanding of the ministers and their services. This is exactly what we suggest you the readers do in the assignment below.

15 Standard Features of an Office

♦ Authority

- Government
- Canon
- Lawmaking
- Legislation
- Organization
- Discipline
- Teaching
- Judging
- Management & Supervision
- Guardianship
- Development
- Officiation of Rites & Sacrament
- Enforcement
- Rule

These 15 actions will be evident and operative in the ministry of every officer on the planet, as well as in the jurisdiction he is assigned to.

Notes:

Special Assignment:

Students are to research first the **46 terms** in the manner they approached **Meaning of an Officer** and **An Officer Is Also**. Assign them next to draft a Ministry Profile of the Officers' work, responsibilities, implied powers, and authority to be shared with their group and discussed in the class.

Suggestion: Have individual students or group captains present profiles to class before discussion.

Validity of Explanation

You may be wondering by now what ground there is to attach such broad powers and duties to these positions, and what place they have in the Church of the Lord Jesus Christ. The answer to question one is on the ground of the 15 features that apply to any office and are thus inherited by its officer. If words mean what they say, and definitions convey meaning, context, intent and usage, then no one who researches the word <u>officer</u> (or office for that matter) can argue with its descriptions. What the positions themselves define for us as their duty, function, approach and purpose, further clarify the Lord's intentions for installing them. For example, as you will find out later, the explanations given for the apostle and prophet, along with their duties, leave no room for doubt regarding their officiates. Investigation of the meanings of the remaining three offices establishes them, as well, in the stead of an office. Repeated careful investigations of words like *rule, authority, directive, government, and discipline* (or *mastery*) kept surfacing. When tracing each word's meaning down to its end, we were inevitably brought back to these basic attributes. The teacher took us to the words *doctor* and *rabbi*. When following this train of definitions, we ended up with discipline, mastery, standards, rule, and principles as their chief influence.

With pastors we ended up with rule, leadership, discipline, training, and nurturing as their primary impact. For the evangelist, we found exploring this officer led us to the roots of didactic that imply teaching, legislating and such. No matter how we probed it, the Ephesians 4:11 posts showed up as offices, and that means official. It spells authority, governance, power, and headship. The word *post* itself is a synonym for office and thus carries the same weight. From our opening discussions on the institutional office of the *Melakim* in Israel, the functions of a deputy, authorized and licensed representatives are clearly seen as the root of the officiations God ordained.

The above information is further borne out by what Ephesians 4:12-16 adds. It states clearly what is expected of the office. Function, role and purpose are succinctly laid out in the passage. Here is a summary of them:

1. *Equipping the saints.* Think about what that calls for.

2. *Work of Ministry*, the object of #1. Consider its demands.

3. *Edifying of the body of Christ.* What involvement does this one require?

The Goals of the Ephesians Five are:

A.   Unity of the faith

B.   Knowledge of Jesus Christ

C.   Perfect Man

D.   Measure and Stature of Christ's Fullness

E.	Advancement from Spiritual Childhood

F.	Wisdom for Stability

G.	Discernment of Doctrine

H.	Protection from Temptation and Seduction

I.	Avoidance of Deception

J.	Instillation of boldly Spoken Truth

K.	Balanced Exposition of Truth with Love

L.	Growth in All Things

M.	Expansion into the Headship of Christ

N.	Full Occupation (and preoccupation) of Each Member of the Body with His mission

O.	Equal Distribution and Execution of Christ's Workload

P.	Unified Efforts and Labors

Q	Uniform Methods and Perspectives

R.	Stimulation of the Body's Growth

S.	Production of the Body's Self-Edification in Love

Suggestion: Have students describe practical operations of **A-S** as an assignment.

Studying these goals, you would find that a range of duties, skills, and applications is required to accomplish them. Yet they can be broken down into discrete categories for achievement:
- ◆ Organization
- ◆ Leadership
- ◆ Education
- ◆ Revelation
- ◆ Discipling

- ♦ Attendance and Care
- ♦ Discipline
- ♦ Government
- ♦ Maturation
- ♦ Preparation

Ten, simple-sounding steps, but oh, what is involved in planning, orchestrating, implementing and administrating them to achieve that 19-point goal list! For that, an office—and nothing less than an office—is needed. The supreme achievement of the officer, as a result of his efforts, is sanctification of the body from sin to the truth of God, and its establishment in His righteousness for inheritance and eternal life.

About An Office

The high point of an office is officialdom. That is the primacy of correctness, propriety, authority, government, and order. Officialdom speaks to structure, organization, execution (follow through), standardization, uniformity, and maintenance (follow up). Regulations, enforcement, and consequences accompany the office. Furthermore, the office includes a staff, facilities, and other resources to see it gets all its missions accomplished. The inclusion of these brings in leadership, management, and administration—spiritual, natural, eternal, and temporal.

An office exists for the execution of a plan, cause, or operation. It is necessary for the maintenance or expansion of a work begun and in need of enlargement by efficiency and excellence. Obedience, cooperation, duty, commitment, responsibility, and accountability all have a part in the assignment of the office. Even so, an office invariably implies a delegation. It is a post, profession, and directorate. It is not a casual or part time occupation.

To stand in an office is to execute that office; to carry out its aims, purposes, activities and operations. It means to see that specific functions are fulfilled. Therefore, initiatives figure prominently in an office, and to prosper, it must integrate a business. An income-producing, expense-generating component must be included to assure economic success and guarantee productive, prosperous outlets for the talents of those engaged (or affected) by it.

Recorders, processors, technicians, buying, selling, management, transmission, conveyance, communication, development, research, reputation, management, planning, directorship, and coordination all make up the elements of the official execution of the affairs and interests of another—the principal definition of an office and its officer. For the Ephesians 4:11 group, the "other" is <u>Christ and His affairs</u>. His officer's activities center on the Church. The mission is the advancement of the Kingdom of God. And the mandate? *"Make ready a people prepared for the Lord."* How? *"Go ye into all the world; preach the gospel; make disciples; baptize and teach disciples, and then equip, stabilize, and unify them."*

Exercise: Take the preceding information and use it to establish the importance, purpose, and functional value of the five-fold. Be explanative and illustrative. **Discuss as a class or study group.**

Chapter One Review

1.   Explain the method the Lord used to teach God's doctrine and to establish His kingdom through the Church.

2.   Explain the link of Psalm 78:1-3 and Isaiah 29:9 to #1.

3.   Discuss the essence of the compensatory accommodations.

4.   What is meant by "Over 50% of human life offerings subsist on what Satan did in the Garden of Eden"?

5.   What did God institute the religious rituals to do?

6.   Discuss Psalm 68:18 in relation to Ephesians 4:11.

7.   Review the teaching on the kind of gifts Christ gave.

8.   Tell how the gifts Christ gave constitute officers.

9.   Address the meanings and weight of an office.

10. Give the importance of knowing the 46 Five-Fold Duty Officiates.

11. The 15 Standard Features of an office are crucial in what 3 significant ways?

12. State what you understand to be the root and origination of the Five-fold Office's power and authority.

13. Compare Ephesians 4:12-16 to what you answered in #12.

14. Clarify the connection between #12 and #13 to the 9 categories for achievement.

15. Why do the officers exist and why must they remain?

16. Draw a brief composite of the work of #15.

17. Summarize the *Melakim* and its similarity to the Ephesians 4 officers.

CHAPTER TWO
One Office per Vessel

One Office Per Vessel

In previous years the doctrine of ministry office universality has taken hold and runs many a ministers astray. Lack of enlightenment has led earlier leaders to believe there is no boundary drawn between the officers and their offices. Since the resources of God are mainly spiritual, popular teachers treat them as non-existent. Believing God sees things as they do—out of sight, out of mind—they educate people to ignore the fundamental premise governing all creation.

No matter what realm of God's handiwork and institutions you study, you will find that boundaries and hierarchy play a predominant role in them all. Every kingdom and its creatures have a built-in signal to alert them to the boundary wall implanted in each one. Physical signals such as limitations, inability, weakness, and the like inform creatures of their natural hierarchy. Natural restrictions sound pain or fatigue alarms to warn a creature that he is overstepping his bounds. Nature adds to these territorial boundaries. These are where climate, terrain, the elements, and indigenous inhabitants all join forces to signal to the wayward wanderer that he has stayed into foreign territory. Early warning signs may be scent traps, barriers, or constructed barricades. Another sign may be subordinate guard. Any number of means could be used to deter an intruder's invasion into another's territory. Seen or unseen, respected or not, boundaries and hierarchy are built into all creation.

Rocks barricade tidewaters, the sun blocks the night. Gravity guards the way to independent human flight to seal the skies from fallen man. The invisible confines the visible; the supernatural, the natural. Spirits stand watch over the delimitations of the flesh to see that the mysterious treasures and privileges of the immortal world are concealed and protected. Every one of God's pathways has a door through which only the licensed and appointed may pass.

It is no different with the concocted institutions of men. They too follow God's order through nature's pattern. Doors, levels, walls, and barriers fix and keep their desired bounds. Guards, alarms, alert, and warning systems all protect space and territory not to be intruded upon. The secret to getting beyond lines and bars that safeguard the preserved, privileged, or private territory lies in several things: Construction, Knowledge, Equipment, License and Codes. These all, combined or separately, must be observed if one would proceed from a common or open space to a restricted one. For the animals their construction is encoded with the knowledge and equipment they need to instinctively advance or be restricted to specific realms and territories. By design they are licensed, or not, to occupy or venture into certain areas. The same is true for the rest of Creation. Ordainments are achieved through design and species. Their environments are blocked or released by the patterns used to make them and the spirit within them that gives them life.

With humans, the ruling principle of architecture and inspiration continue. Musicians, actors, singers, mathematicians, and skilled people of all walks of life can attest to it. You either have it or you don't. You cannot manufacture it and can only slightly imitate it. The gifts and talents are either present or they are not. When it comes to organizational or function hierarchy, mankind is obliged by laws and forces beyond his control to keep within the ruling guidelines set by God. Human makeup, personality and temperament, abilities, and faculty divide and classify humanity. Whether they accept it or not, the greater decisions concerning their existence have been made for them. Practice, frustration, deviousness or any other strategy cannot annul what makeup has predetermined a person is able to do. Based on the manifestations they exhibited to the world, their life's work is cut out for them. The scientist may yearn to be an actor, artist, or singer, but it is his makeup that determines if he can or will succeed at his heart's desire. The teacher may long to entertain; the mathematician may crave a chance at police work, law or medicine. Still, his make up will be a deciding factor. When a person's desires disagree with his makeup, the stronger of the two will settle any conflict *(Study Job 37:7)*.

With the newborn natural child, his gifts and talents inevitably reveal who he is and his life's work. With the born again spiritual child the same is the case. In the way the natural child may yearn to be a great athlete his talents and abilities may say he is a born builder. The signals and controls governing the two fields may disqualify him for his choice. Meanwhile, once a person is saved, his makeup may qualify him for his spiritual call, whereas in the world they did not, or vice-versa. Try as he might, one may strive to be an apostle or a pastor, a leader, or an administrator. Yet his natural talents communicate entirely different messages to his performance abilities. Mental capacities, psychological outlook, physical stamina, even emotional perspective may all say he is oriented toward helps. Leadership aptitude may be lacking the capabilities for the job desired or may be absent. His mental acumen and basic intelligence may all say his desire is incompatible with his makeup. All these may stand up against his will and not supply what he needs when performance is required of him. Lower creatures accept this. Mankind, on the other hand, frequently rejects it in favor of his own will. The church is often like this.

The teachings that have taught the body to ignore or disdain God's ordinations show little comprehension of God and His basic orders. As Jesus said to the Sadducees who challenged him about the afterlife with the woman who had seven husbands, "You do not know the Scriptures, nor the power of God." Modern teachers, too, do not know the Scriptures nor the power of God if they fail to comprehend this simple heavenly truth. Purely carnal and earthly perspectives have confined their insight and reasoning abilities to life under the sun and the world of mortal men. Consequently, a similar attitude causes modernists to teach the Lord's Church to covet what is not theirs and foster frustration and envy in matters that God alone keeps in His control.

To compound the problem, the boundaries and hierarchy we have been discussing are contained in the requisites for the offices or ministry positions. The demands of the position coupled with the need they fill and the purpose for which they were created all determine the makeup of the one to fill it. Pastors have specific functions. They possess the attributes, attitudes, skills, abilities, capability, and capacity to assure the job is well understood and performed. Often their life experiences further enhance the others to see that they and their abilities meet the challenges of the work they are ordained to. With the others it is the same. Each officer must "have what it takes." If he doesn't, he will fail, the work will suffer; and the plans, purpose, and mission of the Lord will be frustrated.

Besides all that is the matter of understanding the office and their functionaries. A functionary is an official representative with rights, responsibilities, and privileges. He is an operator who handles the affairs of his principal. The functionary is deputized by his principal with proxy authority and assured by the nature and terms of the covenant that his actions will be backed up by the principal. He serves as the principal's steward or instrument and is used to set in order, organize, structure, and activate whatever the principal needs done but is unable to attend to personally.

As you can see from the explanation given, no one can arbitrarily decide to put himself in a principal's affairs without being assigned, and certainly not without asking first. Human leaders don't hire unqualified or incompatible functionaries and neither will God. Therefore, the notion that anyone can choose or fulfill adequately and competently the office of his desire is false. The simple ability to carry a tune does not designate one a singer. To be argumentative or a debater does not constitute a lawyer. Thus, more than teaching a subject is needed to make a teacher. A pastor is required to do much more than attract a following. The prophet must be able to do more than see in the Spirit and utter words under the Spirit's influence. The evangelist needs to be able to do more than preach; and the apostle, more than found a work. All these offices have broad and varied functions that call for specific skills and abilities. Knowledge, intelligence, equipment, orientation, faculties, and capacity must line up with the natural resources a person possesses for appointment and license to be conferred.

In later discussions, the aptitudes and so forth, a minister's needs for a particular office are defined at length. From them you can determine if you are in the right office or suited for ministry you would like to have. When thinking about the E-4 office Paul unveils, you must separate the office's mission from its purpose to see the achievement of that mission. Then you must identify the divine goal and objective of every effort and activity the mission requires for its purpose. Afterward, you should examine the position's description, its overall duties, fundamental responsibilities, and basic officiations and executions. Before you enter it you should be reasonably able to cite these in their broad context. Next, you should reflect an understanding of how you fit in the scheme of God's plan for your office and your particular service. Following, you should display a comprehension of the impact you and your work will have on the body; generally speaking. Lastly, you should have a good idea of how your personal ministry methods, views, and activities will affect those you reach and teach for God. Some means of answering these questions should be sought out and addressed before you step into that office you want so much for God to appoint you to.

Based on all the variables and critical factors discussed, you can easily see the problem with the popular idea that every minister can stand in any office he chooses at once. If the equipment is not there, then the prospects for success are nil.

Chapter Two Review

1. What is meant by the phrase "one office per vessel?"

2. What three areas of God's Creation convey the answer to # 1 above?

3. Explain what is meant by barriers, blocks, and barricades in respect to # 1.

4. Research and state what a boundary is.

5. Research and state what a hierarchy is.

6. Describe a function and distinguish it from an operation.

7. Define functionary and give an example of him.

8. Discuss human delimitations.

9. Relate # 8 to the E-4 offices.

10. List the things 7-10 need to perform.

11. Discuss the premise on which one may be qualified or disqualified for # 9.

CHAPTER THREE
Characteristics of Offices and Personalities

Characteristics of Offices and Personalities

What a Characteristic Is

The information contained in this section applies to all the officers and should be referred to from time to time to refresh your memory on the importance of the officers and the benefit of knowing their identifying features. It will be helpful to you in recognizing the various representations witnessed in an officer's ministry as compared to the work he is doing. A conflict between two could signal a servant's misapplication of his or her gifts, or a misjudgment of his or her call.

A characteristic is a distinguishing mark or feature that sets one thing apart from another. It is also a trait or collection of traits that so identifies what a thing or person is that it makes a reliable instrument of recognition. In discussing the Five-fold Officers, the characteristics that set one apart from the other are consequential. This is so especially in light of modern teachings on the subject. If you read the previous material carefully, you understand that the features that make one a prophet, an apostle, or any one of the other officers of the church are inborn. They have been implanted in the person's seed and thus influence his designed makeup, even before the world was founded. The significance of these engraftings has to do with solid recognition ability.

The church, God has so ordained, must be able to recognize her leaders. She must be able to say with reasonable certainty who is the apostle, who is the prophet, who is the pastor, etc., and why. Her discoveries must be based on more than a word from the Spirit or a repetitive unction in principle; not that these are unreliable sources for revelation. If, however, the Lord's intent was to have us exclusively look to our individual inner feelings and perceptions about these professional matters pertaining to His church, He would not have moved the scribes to pen the Scriptures. Apparently, the Lord found fault with our relying solely on our private interpretations and understanding of the inward unction, as a Body, to verify the placement and eligibility of our leaders.

The fault God found was with the instability of human responses. God saw that circumstances, external influences, even physical maladies could distort our perspectives. What was clear to us yesterday or last week, today, for any reason, may not be so clear. When it comes to judging the officers of the church, this is especially true. A number of things can trigger error or cause one to recant a declaration of who and what a person is in the Body, and in what stead he is to minister. Aside from those just mentioned, other reasons may be strife, envy, a rift due to arguments, favoritism; or just plain dislike for the person to stand in a particular office. Simple lack of information or education on the subject can be the culprit. You can probably add a few more to this list yourself.

The point of this discussion is human nature. It is unreliable for many reasons. This being the case, the task of identifying the church's officers and other ministers is risky without sound documentation upon which to base one's observations and conclusions.

The Apostle Peter was convinced of this by the Holy Spirit and wrote in his second epistle that the surest word of prophecy could only come from the Holy Scriptures. Having already been committed to paper, there was little chance of the factors that invalidated spontaneous human perception affecting them, once they made their accurate way to a person's memory and heart. Reading the Bible repeatedly to refresh one's memory to recall God's truth on a subject allows one to recommit to memory what was forgotten or distorted over time. You might ask, what has this to do with the characteristics and features of those who stand in the Ephesians 4:11 offices? The answer is plenty. The Bible arduously goes through the trouble to define what it deems is acceptable character, credentials of eligibility for the people who will oversee the flock of God. What is equally important, when we talk about recognizing those who rule over us, as the word says, is knowing what to look for and how to weigh our conclusions about them. The ability to do this is critically important for pastors, as they are most vulnerable to the problems erroneous identification can cause.

Pastors are the ones who open their churches and expose their flocks to the itinerant officers of the church. A mistake in judgment could be devastating to those in their charge. Therefore, the information contained in this section can prove invaluable in protecting the flock from the ravenous wolves who stalk it for prey. The discussion to follow on characteristics and features can go a long way toward helping pastors guard their flocks.

There are, first of all, certain telltale characteristics possessed by all the officers. Those who are destined to minister in a leadership capacity in the Body all display consistent attitudes, outlooks, and approaches to Christianity, its life and problems. In much the same way a police officer can be recognized (in or out of uniform) by his viewpoints and convictions many times, God's ministers too can be discerned by others in the Body—and sometimes by those who are not. Bypassing physical looks, body build, language dialects, even nationality, the Lord's deposits in a person for eventual service to Him emit a common fragrance. The call to minister is lodged in the spirit and is exuded through the basic makeup of the "called one."

There is a commonality in temperament, for example. Viewpoints on like issues may be strikingly similar. Comments about religious matters, God, the church, even the people who make up the church, are usually shared by the same group and discerned by outsiders as well. Ministry emphases, development focuses, and outlooks on how to sanctify, refine, educate and mature the church may be comparable as a universal stream of thought becomes evident among different groups. The apostle may see it this way; the pastor may not. The evangelist is convinced this is the most important thing; the teacher disagrees. The prophet says that all is needed is "so and so;" the others see it differently. Previously these perspectives were seen as hotbeds of contention. Today they can be used as guides to diversity. That is what this material seeks to bring about.

The analyses to come do not take into account whether the person serves the Lord Jesus Christ or not. Since the attributes in question are endowed before the womb, salvation and Christ have little to do with their common equipment for God's call; neither does what they do with that call upon answering it.

As you prepare to go through the outlines to come, here are some considerations you may want to think on. Ask yourself, what is it about a prophet's spirit (a term used by Paul in the Bible) that enables its presence to be readily detected by the discerning eye. Take, for example, the woman at the well. What did Jesus do to cause her to see Him as a prophet? How is it one can quickly spot an evangelist? What about the teacher? What manner does he portray that causes one to ask if he teaches? Similarly, the pastors—how are they recognized? What is it they do or say that gives them away? Deacons in the church have even been recognized outside of Sunday service. The acute eye can spot them in an instant. How? Why? These questions are going to be answered in the discussions to come as the distinctives that reveal and classify one officer over another are explored. Obviously, the Lord implanted certain characteristic abilities to enable us to discern who was who and to enable the minister for his service to God. The analyses are to point us in the direction of His implantations and gifts, and away from personal bias, private interpretation, or other factors that ignore God's handiwork; they can induce us to reject His will in favor of our prejudices and preferences. Prior to getting into those characteristics we spoke of, we want to digress for a moment to help set your mind for them. Most particularly, we want to give you a firm ground for the largely ignored, deeply submerged officer of the five. It is the office of the apostle.

Recent years have the winds of change warning us that God is about to resurface and highly project this officer into the mainstream of His church. A Prophetic Move is undoubtedly to be followed by an Apostolic Move. With the stigma attached to the office, and Satan's utter intimidation by him, the likelihood of confusion and raging debate have already begun to take shape. Sides are being taken and battle gear is being donned. Is there any such thing as an apostle today? If so, what does he do? On it goes. How can one tell an apostle today? Where does he fit in the modern scheme of things? How much authority does he have? Who is to listen to him—who needs him for that matter? The struggle with this one officer is immense. Many do not favor a resurrection of this mantle, as if they could dictate to God. Pastors cringe at the idea of having this high-ranking officer of the church reinstated. Most have made up their minds to simply ignore him; maybe he will just go away. Power brokers in the ministry have begun to take advantage of the church's naiveté and have embarked on campaigns to delude the uninformed into thinking they are their apostle. Frustrated pastors who love the Lord are not willing to disobey Him, but find themselves in an enormous tug of war over the welfare of the precious sheep God has entrusted into their care. Perhaps this material will address some of the controversy and hopefully relieve the discomfort being felt by those who know the apostle is coming, but simply don't know what to do with him when he (or she) arrives.

It is for these reasons the apostle is treated more extensively in this book than any of the other officers. Nevertheless, it is recommended that you obtain my book, to get a comprehensive teaching on the subject. Excerpts from it will be used here from time to time. However, the fullest understanding will be gained from studying the separate text. Likewise the Prophet too is treated sparingly, giving less attention than them all. The reason for this is the same. A thorough treatment of the Prophet's Mantle is given in my book, "Constructing the Contemporary Prophet." It is published by Kendall Hunt Publishers, Dubuque Iowa.

To ready the church to deal with the apostle and his counterfeits, the following material was developed. An overview of the office's origin, purpose, and fundamental functions precedes the study. It gives you the underlying concept of the official and shows how and why Christ renamed His chosen twelve apostles on the mountain centuries ago. A brief discussion of the anointing, a chief ministry faculty, precedes the discussion.

Chapter Three Review

1.   Tell the value of understanding characteristics in relation to the five-fold?

2.   What is a characteristic and what is its most important function?

3.   What must the Church do to accurately recognize her leaders?

4.   What is the problem with relying strictly on human senses?

5.   Name the importance of recognizing Church leaders, and how is it best done?

6.   Discuss the telltale characteristics all five-fold share.

7.   List the considerations given for the five-fold outlines.

8.   What is the significance of the Lord's implantations to their office characteristics?

9.   The Prophetic Move is followed by what? Why?

10.   Explain #9 above.

CHAPTER FOUR
The Apostle

The Apostle

The Apostle is the first of our five offices. What is an apostle? What makes one an apostle? What is *not* an apostle? What do modern apostles do? In this section, as we individually address each subject of the Five-fold Officers of the New Testament Church of Jesus Christ, questions like these will be studied and answered to help the Lord advance His program for end time revival, new creation cultivation, and fulfillment of the Scriptures.

An apostle is, in a sentence, *a special messenger*. More precisely, he is a specially commissioned messenger. In the Christian church, he is sent by the Lord Jesus Christ. The Apostle is the most remarkable and stringently used minister of the church. What makes him remarkable is that he is, of necessity, the most highly endowed and endued of the church's officials; and for good reason. The process of reaping and garnering souls, establishing disciples in the kingdom and sanctifying them from the world for God begins with the apostle. There are a number of sound, wise reasons for this. None of them have as their motive the exaltation of flesh, or the ascension of one human being over another. God's reasons are strictly expediency, and they all stem from His orderliness.

God is order. All of His creation was made and ordained to respond to and function within certain invariable orders. His absolute perfection means that at the outset, what He did was perfect and not in need of future variation or revision. Since He made no mistake, there is never any reason for Him to alter His original approaches and methods. Keep this in mind and you will, from this moment on, have no problem with the increased endowments of the apostle or any of the officers. You will not find yourself envious of, or insecure over, the graded dispensations given the remaining officers and the other members of the Body of Christ for their respective services either.

Getting back to God's perfect orders, when it came to the organization of His church He stayed consistent with what He had already set in motion. The laws of creation, origination, and reproduction all pertain to the church equally, as they do to creation. The preeminence of prophecy heads the list. Genesis tells us that God does everything by His word. He merely speaks and it is so. Once the Father's word goes forth, the Holy Spirit performs its works. Also, from the moment God created man, He began to use vessels to accomplish on earth what He originated in the spirit according to the following principles. For God the rule is:

- The word precedes the move of the Spirit
- Spirit precedes the movement of the flesh
- The heavenly precedes the activation of the earthly
- Supernatural precedes the natural
- Seed precedes fruit
- Eternity preempts temporality
- A heavenly pattern designs an earthly plan

♦ The order is heaven down, not from the earth up

Essentially, these sum up the progressions and actuations of God. He kept to these principles up to and including what it took to bring man back to His Creator. For this, God sent His Son.

The Decision to Use the Apostle

The first apostle was a "sent one". The very first "Sent One" was sent from heaven to earth to redeem humanity back to God. I Corinthians 15 calls Him the Lord from heaven and the Spiritual Man. The principle was set in motion: a spiritual man must be apostled to go with power and spirit to snatch the chosen elect out of the hands of Satan and the bowels of sin. The power of the enemy, humanity's captor being devastating, required no less than that which a deputized Commissioned One (whose Commissioner is God) could possess. The Sent One would have been face to face with the God of the covenant, and had been literally touched by the mighty hand that would wrought His victories. He would have to know God's truth, as it alone could defeat the lie. He would have to be better in all respects than the enemy He was to confront and conquer, winning the respect and trust of the captives as He did so. Also, the Apostle would have official access to the secrets of heaven and its treasuries to finance and under gird His work sufficiently enough to persuade the lost and bound that He was truly sent by the Father of Abraham. A study of John's Gospel will establish that Jesus met this criteria perfectly.

The Stringent Use of the Apostle

Key to the apostle's potency in ministry is his extraordinary, yet necessary empowerment. The apostle contains within himself the fullness of all the dispensation and impartations to come from his ministry.

In addition, the apostle (sent one) would, unequivocally, be capable of penetrating the holds and caverns of darkness to bring humanity to the heart and throne of God. The order of the prophet had already been settled. His anointing would not do; neither would that of a priest alone. They are sent to those who have known God or have heard of Him. The prophet has been established as the mouth of the Lord to, or on behalf of, the covenanted ones for generations, and the priest their established teacher. All that was instituted to put them in effect has been determined and in operation since before the foundation of the world. No, the special messenger would have to have the combined capabilities and capacities of both and more besides.

Since he would have to speak to (and combat) the gods of the nations, seize their very kingdoms, and put their principalities off their thrones to establish the kingdom of God, he needs to be a prophet with unprecedented power. His work with the redeemed to see they did not revert back to their pagan roots and orientation, but became the sanctified children of God, called for a priest. To establish the new kingdom; to equip the redeemed for divine service; to guard the flock called for a pastor; to fulfill the charge of Matthew 28:19 and Jeremiah 3:15. By all means, the apostle must not neglect to teach the redeemed the government and ways of their new kingdom. That would call for a teacher. To see that the lost continued to hear the gospel and have opportunity to enter the kingdom of God and inherit the salvation of Christ required an evangelist whose anointed gifts for preaching would initiate the program in the first place. With all this, he was to be a missionary as well. Oh, but the true apostle is much, much more than that.

Our sent one must be all these and be able to fulfill every heavenly and ecclesiastical rank to lead the armies of the Living God. He must be able to interact and cooperate with the heavenly hosts, to officiate, to be a magistrate over the divine kingdom of new creation saints and to adjudicate their controversies. Our Sent One must be nurturing to develop and mature the church for their eternal place with the Savior. His wisdom must feed and enlighten them with the word of truth and train and employ the called out ones in God's institutions and industry. Yes, this sent one would have to be as heavily endowed as he was heavily charged. As you can see from the brief descriptions given above, the apostle's mandate and the modernist missionary's mandate are worlds apart. Nevertheless, the apostle's calls include the dispatch to a mission as God calls them to spearhead and dominate His new moves.

Christ established it, the first apostles executed it; and as long as sin, the flesh, and Satan all remain the same, and God unchangeable, the reasons for "sent ones" will continue to exist.

With such demanding responsibilities, thought the Godhead, We must create another officer who can handle this business with the containment of the prophet and priest to be our sent one; one whose special construction will lend itself well to the mission and whose peculiar orientation can withstand the fiercest demonic onslaught and overcome it to conquer and free the prisoners assigned to him. He must, to be successful, incorporate all the others and be suited to the needs and conflicts of the generations to come. He must be protective of the purchased possession; responsive to us; and zealously determined to finish his assignment, they concluded.

More importantly, since his charge is great, his power and authority too must be equally as great; otherwise, our sent one will fail and the souls will not be delivered. Where could such power be entrusted? What kind of human could be faithful enough to remain loyal, and how will We assure it?, said the Lord. To assure absolute obedience, essential for success and humility, he must be fitted with special restraints that will enable him to be abnormally accessible to the Godhead and compelled to devotion and allegiance. Our first sent one will be the father of many. This group we will call the apostle because they will be the secret weapon: the peculiar instruments of God in human form.

The discussion did not take place on earth, but in heaven. It did not occur in time, but in eternity. The decision was made before the spirits and souls of mankind were created. It took place while they were still on the drawing board of creation as God was viewing the events of His human race, before they left His Being, and providing the solutions to them. It was then that the deposits were ordained and made, when the officers were determined, and their endowments dispensed. The apostle was made the apostle, the prophet was made the prophet, and so on. All of it was to take place when the work of the Son was completed. By Adam's birthday, all the details were resolved. The Master's Plan was activated, the courses were set and could not be altered or stopped. All the intricacies were intermeshed and nothing could undo the perfect plan. The power of "predestiny" receiving its sovereign from eternity was quickened. History was in the making, and God's business of bringing His word and will to pass began.

The Apostle and the Plan of Redemption

The Plan of Redemption stipulated that by man sin came, so by man sin must be overturned (1 Corinthians 15:21-22). This, we all know, God did in the incarnation of His Son Jesus Christ. To redeem His lost creation from the clutches of sin caused by Adam, God needed a "sent one," an apostle. The Bible has taught us the "sent one," God's very first Apostle (God is always first; He sets in motion, not responds to, what takes place on earth—that is what makes Him forever, Alpha and Omega), was Jesus His Son. When Christ came to earth He came from heaven dispatched by the Father to exercise divine authority, exert surrender and obedience upon the devil, and to loose the bonds of captivity from His children. The condition of the chosen elect, then, was that they were lost in trespasses and sins, bound in idolatrous practices, and did not know the Lord God of their covenant. Israel had mainstreamed, to their destruction, with the nations around them and was duped into thinking they served Jehovah through their paganistic rituals. Sounds a great deal like today, doesn't it?

Conditions Ripe For Apostolic Ministry

The Apostolic Ministry emerges and thrives under certain conditions. In these times its presence is demanded and its powers greatly felt. Following is a description of the conditions ripe for this ministry. It is presented from a historical standpoint couched within contemporary overtones.

The Law of the Lord had become buried under the rubble of human religiosity and those who really sought the God of Abraham could not find Him because of the godless gatekeepers that blocked the way to true salvation: namely, the Pharisees, the Sadducees, the Scribes, and the Lawyers. The candle of revelation had gone out and the people thought everything was acceptable if they said it was for God. Crime riddled the nation, and they were enslaved to the very kingdoms they yearned to emulate. Israel was a servant to the cruel master and could no longer discern the true from the false, her God from the gods of the heathens. Her original faith was splintered and there were numerous sects rising up saying they were the way. Yet the sheep of God's flock were daily slaughtered; the provisions of the covenant were being withheld as a result. Blessings were being denied and the people saw their religious leaders as their God. Such was the state of the nation during Jesus' time.

Sickness, disease, and despair were intensified by quackery, selfishness and greed. The flock was a constant prey and no one sought the lost, bound up the bruised, or set at liberty them that were imprisoned by the forces of darkness. Supernatural signs were counterfeited as a throwback to the days when the Lord Jehovah really moved among His people; when He showed Himself strong with great signs and wonders.

To keep the people's eyes on those manufacturing their religious beliefs and practices, an occultic move was instigated to rival the true God. Baal prophets and priests performed religious services and signs and miracles for the people. In fact, the nation of God began to be trained by sinners. The evil and the wicked became tutors of the righteous and redeemed. Now the supernatural was in the hands of, and performed by, the sons and agents of darkness. Occultism had succeeded in savagely taking hold in the nation of Jehovah. Read about Jeroboam, Ahab, and Jezebel in the Old Testament, and the seven sons of Sceva in the Book of Acts. These three spawned the seeds that ensnared and eventually downed the nation. Humanism had seeped into their culture and became their ruin. Also research Omri in Micah 6:16.

Sound familiar? It should. The world described as ripe for a sent one begged for an Apostolic Move. It has since then repeated itself throughout history. The Judge System of ancient Israel recounts it best: "Everyone did what was right in his own eyes." Although Deuteronomy 12 condemns this attitude, it has become strongly rooted in the church of today. In our modern world it is no different. Polytheism is dogging the heels of what was once a monotheistic society. Pseudo Christianity has desecrated the holy habitation of God. Artificial religion has displaced, for the most part; that which Christ descended from heaven to install for man.

The world's education system is lord and the Christian minister's acceptance is decreed by non-Christians—unbelievers. God's servants are clamoring at the ivy halls of men to receive their anointing for religious service. They are intoxicated by humanism and fail to realize that anointing from men cannot qualify them for God's service. Although the conditions are taken from cases recorded in ancient history, the works of darkness will always see that at the same time history will always mirror current events.

It was against this dismal backdrop that the Lord called out Abram, raised up Moses, commissioned Josiah, prophesied the Coming One and incarnated His Son. As it was with Moses in bringing Israel out of Egypt (a type of the flesh and the world), so it was when the Christ was born and when the first apostles were commissioned. Restricting the need for the apostle to no more than a divinely inspired voyager is to ignore all the reasons Moses was sent, all the reasons Christ was sent, and all the reasons Jesus saw fit to endow and send twelve men to found and to keep His church. Those twelve were the seeds of a perpetual apostolic regime intended to guard and ground the church until Jesus returned.

What Apostles Do

Only one, and at the most three, apostles could have been used to spread the gospel and found the church. After their work was established, they could fall back on others to continue their labors. Beyond that, once the church was founded, each apostle by early theological explanations and restrictive definitions would have outlived his usefulness and rightfully should have retired from duty; or at the least, ceased to use the title. As we all know, this did not happen. The apostles continued in their positions until their deaths. In the meantime they groomed other apostles to succeed them, and their successors did likewise to fulfill the Lord's command and to finish His work. They continued working until they died. But doing what? Seven answers to this question are listed below:

1. With great power giving witness to the resurrection of the Lord Jesus, Acts 4:33.

2. Administering doctrine and solidifying fellowship, Acts 2:43.

3. Provoking fear on opposers and guarding the church, Acts 2:43.

4. Working supernatural signs and wonders to turn people from Satan to

   God, Acts 2:43.

5. Judging sin in the church and governing it, Acts 5:1-11.

6. Teaching the word of God, illuminating Old Testament prophecies with revelations from the New Testament teachings of Jesus Christ, Acts 6:4.

7. Exposing heresy, guarding the truth, Acts chapter 15.

8. Preparing and empowering other ministers.

9. Keeping the Bible truth of God in Christ vivid in church service and worship.

10. Manifesting accurately the truth of God generation to generation,
    2 Corinthians 4:2.

Needless to say, there are many more reasons for the apostle to exist in every generation. In my book, I cite no less than 85 biblical reasons to support the presence and operation of the Apostolic Mantle in every era of man. Again, as long as sin continues to be born in man, Satan remains the god of this age and the god of this world, and God Most High stays the immutable God who never changes, the offices of Ephesians 4:11 will always be needed and staffed. From time to time, though, they will fade in and out of the Church's foreground and as need determines, recede from the spotlight.

Why Apostles Are Few

The most limited number of officers to fill an office in any generation is the apostle. While they may be present in every age, for the reasons stated above, they will vary from period to period in volume. Once the force of apostles needed to found and to ground a new move of God, to found His latest sanctified institutions, and to staff them with the remaining five-fold officers has been completed, the emphasis on the apostle will shift to the pastors, teachers, and evangelists for maintenance. The prophet's office remains vibrant and well staffed to see that God's fresh words continue to flow to the generations, and that interpretations of ancient truth are unfolded in the eras in which they must apply.

The apostle, on the other hand, fades into the background until the new move he officiated begins to corrode with the doctrines of men, seducing spirits, and humanist religion. Each time this happens, the Church of Jesus Christ, as Scripture defines it, ceases to exist. Hence, resurrection of the apostle's mantle becomes necessary to "call out" the "called out ores" who cease to be separated from sin; who no longer light the darkness; and whose salt no longer preserves the earth. When the lamp set upon the hill gets snuffed out under the basket of worldliness and sin, then the apostle will be called upon by God to step forward from the shadows to restore and re-establish the true church of the Living God. This pattern is seen in three ancient Old Testament Apostolic Shadows. Here is why.

Church Takeover

Short sighted, narrow perspective teachers have failed to understand that when the church, by definition, ceases to be separated, they are no longer God's church. Thus the work of evangelism becomes a matter of prostelyzing as the gospel God delivered is no longer what is preached. Its dilution by the world means the Holy Spirit, who cannot honor a lie, can no more birth sons and daughters into the kingdom of God when the word of God, which sets Him in motion, is no longer being preached. No new babes means unsaved sinners fill the pews, and the righteous are scattered or now shepherded by those who are not Christ's but Satan's. The greater part of the church, then, is not the Body of Christ, but becomes another "religious world institution." The Book of Revelation establishes that this cycle will continue until the final days of earth and man. The continuation automatically says the apostle will continue to be called by the Lord Jesus.

Furthermore, when the insidious tactic of redefinition takes hold, sin is no longer sin, and friendship with the world is condoned. When the Bible is subjugated to the sway of polity, "my way" religion takes precedence over God's way, and worst of all, when the Holy Spirit becomes a principle and no longer a practical and welcome guest in church, a takeover has happened. The church is no longer God's but man's. It is then a sent one (or sent ones) must be raised up to go and take back for God what was stolen, much like humanity in the Garden of Eden, Israel in Egypt and Rome, and the church in the world. The apostles of the age must exert supernatural power and exercise heavenly authority to once more call out those who have melded with the world church and forsaken the true and living God and His only Savior Jesus Christ.

Who and What the Apostle Is

The word itself, we know well by now, means fundamentally a sent one. It describes one sent with extraordinary power on a mission, a delegation, on behalf of another, for a commissarial assignment. Unlike what the church is accustomed to thinking about an apostle, a mission is only one part of his mantle. The word "mission" itself needs to be explained as its misapplication has stripped, and made light of, the office and its officers. The erroneous use of the word has narrowed the scope of the apostolic mandate so strictly as to cause the apostle to be a relegated officer of the remaining five-fold instead of the delegated head of them all. The damage done to the church and the deprivation experienced by the world is immeasurable as the absence of this mighty warrior of the Lord's provisions for His church and man is sorely felt by every strata of society.

A Mission

Before we delve deeper into the contrasts between the apostle and the missionary, attention should be given to the word "mission." A *mission* involves a number of things; among them is ministry. It is a ministry of ambassadorship, meaning the sent one is dispatched to a foreign field to handle the affairs, settle the accounts, and negotiate agreements (which almost always includes peace terms and commerce pacts) in the best interests of the one who sent him. The missionary is invariably lower in rank and authority than the sender and therefore is delegated corresponding powers and authorities to act by proxy in the commissioner's behalf. Generally, the dispatched one is not part of the established orders of the organization, but an outgrowth of its new or special needs. He usually operates outside of the routine to execute and officiate a new thing the organization is doing.

Apostles Are More than Missionaries

Ambassadorship is central to the missionary's position, as is the representation of the sending organization. While a missionary may also be an apostle, missionary journeys do not constitute the apostolic mantle. Missionaries are not always, nor necessarily, apostles. To conclude they are simply because their duties include going on missionary journeys is to state that every ambassador is an apostle. Of course, the idea of that is ludicrous. Even so, by definition, the church is establishing that anyone who goes on a mission trip is automatically an apostle. Even more impossible to accept is that for one to go on a church approved missionary journey, they must first become or be recognized as an apostle. Can this be true? Is it so? It is if one accepts without question the fundamental definition of an apostle given by the church today. Who would dare make such an inane statement and give it the credence of canon? No one we know and respect for sure; yet that is precisely what popular doctrine has us believing. True, it is not said outright, or directly taught, that all missionaries are automatically apostles. Nevertheless, exploring accepted teachings thoroughly, the conclusion would be the same unless one enlarged the over simplified definition of what an apostle really is. To leave the matter's clarification to traditional dogma is to severely undermine the Apostle's Mantle and to frustrate the designed and intended orders of God in His moves in the earth.

The Apostle as a Sent One

The sent one designation traditionally applied to the apostle implies some very discrete and potent things. Particularly seen in them is what is contained in the words "delegate, commission, agent, proxy, authority and license," to name but a few. We will examine these terms as they pertain to the apostle briefly here to help lay a definitive foundation for what you are to learn from these teachings. We will start with the word delegate.

An apostle is a delegate of the kingdom of God. Obviously, the foreign field he is sent to by the Lord is the kingdom of men. As a delegate, the apostle is deputized with certain powers and privileges that allow him to act largely independent of his Commissioner's direct involvement. This being true, you can be sure that the apostle's training, pruning, orders, and orientation have more than satisfied any concern over his fidelity, integrity, and allegiance. You can see why only a select few humans can be so trusted by the Lord Jesus Christ with such unbridled latitude in service.

If you did a study of all the implications to be found in just the word "delegate" alone, you would greatly open up your understanding of how "mission" as employed in the Bible broadly enlarges the church's present concept of the apostle's office. It adds the dimension of commission. More than an errand or assignment, it is a literal extension of the reach, power, and authority of the "sent one." For instance, biblically speaking, "a delegate is a representative deputized to a particular service, duty or cal." Of necessity, the idea of delegation is saturated with connotations of power, authority, and rulership. Not only on the part of the delegate is this true, but on behalf of the one who deputized him as well. Such is the case with the Apostolic Commission. Jesus led the scribes of Scripture, under the unction of the Holy Spirit, to take great pains to select words that would, in an instant, convey the all-inclusive idea of the offices and the officers He had in mind when He gave those gifts unto men. Saul of Tarsus, later named Paul the Apostle, was one of those scribes.

The Apostle Paul's Credibility

Paul the Apostle, no one would dispute, was a highly educated man. His stated record of accomplishment could be rivaled by few of his contemporaries. God's choice of him was not casual, nor was it incidental; it was causal. The Lord deliberately brought Paul through his life's path for the purpose for which he was made. Writing the better portion of the New Testament was a large part of that purpose. Using him to define the divine institutions and executions of

His Father was another. Only a man who had known power, position, status, and authority could comprehend the concepts of church and kingdom leadership that Paul elaborated for us in the Bible. His scholarly background coupled with his meticulous approach to everything made him a more than suitable transcriber of the spiritual truths the Lord Jesus revealed to him. The initial epistles contain much of that truth. Paul's personal integrity, loyalty to Christ, and attention to precision all joined together to see that he wrote what Jesus said, using words that accurately communicated what Jesus meant. Paul knew words, he understood hierarchy, and grasped conclusively the fundamental elements of power—all power in general. It is with this vast breadth of wisdom and experience that he penned the distinctives of the five-fold offices and their officers, and detailed scrupulously the particulars of the Apostle's Ministry.

Unbiased, he unveiled its powers and its perils; its trials and triumphs; its authorities and atrocities. Alongside its glories, in the very same breath almost, the apostle depicts the agonies of the office. One phrase has him capsulizing it best: it is found in the book of 2 Corinthians. He says, "trials abound in ministry." Paul did not glamorize the office but solemnly warned those who would stand in it. This was no naive author or historian seeking to immortalize himself in print. Here was a humble, devoted guardian and revealer of truth of the hidden mysteries and eternal ranks of God. He diligently searched and compared words and phrases so as to impart the fullness of what the Son of God wanted His generations of disciples to know and to understand. To look at some of the things he well understood about the institution he was appointed to found and ground as the church of the Lord Jesus Christ, just focus on his word choices. Focus, with and without your religious hat or theological prejudices, and you will discover the wealth of knowledge our founding father left us to introduce and explain the marvelous entity we are part of. Take, to begin with, the word "commission."

The Power of Commission

A "commission" is most basically a written paper giving certain powers, privileges and duties to its bearer or the one named therein. It contains a warrant to confirm and verify the "sent one." The warrant outlines the reason the person is sent, the purpose for their mission, and the legal limits of their rights, privileges, and proxy actions. The Commission Letter from the sending one attests to the sent one's authenticity. Its warrant serves the special function of backing the authority of the one who is sent, or the delegate.

The Commissioner's Warrant defines the delegate's license to act and certifies the veracity of his service. In the warrant are prescriptions for conduct and substantiation of deeds and testimonies that corroborate fully their scope of duties and surety. The written order gives the rank and range of authority the officer has. By the way, wherever there is a mission, there is an officer of an armed force, a nation, or a kingdom which he represents. Officer and mission go hand in hand. The nature of warrant designed by the commissioner serves to establish the delegate with the commission as an agent and vows to support and uphold the legal activities of his ministry during the designated term of his mission.

Furthermore, a commission encompassing a delegation dispenses rights of enactments, authorities to be exercised, and contains entrustments the officer is permitted to utilize and enjoy. A commission is the direct result of an appointment or election to perform certain accomplishments much like that of an agency. The orders, in summary, authorize, empower, and activate the delegate's service; and say to the citizens of the foreign land or field and its government that the sent one is not alone and is acting with the full backing of the power that commissioned him.

Recalling the earlier movies of medieval times and before, to further clarify this concept, one need only remember how dispatched noblemen, lords, and rulers were sent by the king or queen bearing letters that told who they were and why they were sent. The letters detailed what they could do upon arrival at their destination. Going back into the Scriptures you would find that the dispatched messengers of that day did the same thing. Think about the account of Ezra and Nehemiah. When Cyrus the king wanted to authorize their rebuilding efforts, he did so through the letters he wrote to the magistrates over the area where they would be working. The letters were commissions and accomplished the aims we have been discussing on the king's behalf. They proved effective in frustrating the campaign the opposers of the restoration of Judaism led against the two men. When the opposers wanted to thwart the labors of the Jews they tried numerous schemes. After having them all fail, they resorted to writing a false report to the king to have him overturn his original edict. However, as long as the king supported their building program, his letter protected and authorized their work and compelled support from those in authority over the territory where the work was taking place. The point to be gotten from this example is that the original commission given by the king could only be overturned by a written letter superseding his initial edict. Jesus has never overturned, revoked, or vacated His original apostolic edict.

Herein is the importance of the commission letter. It certifies the person given the charge is ready for service and is faithful in the use of their powers, fully defining their investments and endowments. It attests they have been found scrupulous in the execution of their orders and able to not only perform the duties of their command, but to be relied upon to perpetuate the movement of the founder or power that sent them. They are, therefore, accorded equivalent powers and handed jurisdictions to watch over. The commissioned ones have committed themselves to total involvement in the organization they represent and to dutifully support and guard its role in the affairs of the territory they have been dispatched to. No part time jobs here. It is a total immersion in the cause or nothing at all. There is no such thing as a part time Apostolic Ministry.

Whatever is required to carry out the mission of the founder or head, the commissioned ones or sent ones have pledged to do. Moreover, they have bound themselves to allegiance to their commission, and thusly enjoy a great deal of conferred power and the like for the agency they expedite.

The Apostolic Ministry

An Apostolic Ministry is an assignment. No Scripture best captures the spirit of the Apostolic Ministry than Acts 26:18. Imagine what Paul comprehended from the teachings and revelations of his Savior to make him condense the vast responsibility given him in but a few concrete words. (#1)

- To open their eyes (mankind)

- To turn them from darkness to light

- To turn them from the power of Satan to God
...that they may receive forgiveness of sins
...that they may receive an inheritance with the sanctified ones

The above aptly sums up the substance of God's institution of the five-fold offices, among which the apostle is the forerunner and the catalyst.

The missionary may take food and aid, provide recovery and rescue treatment, and even establish schools to execute a teaching mandate, but nowhere near what an apostle is called for is a missionary intended by God to do. An apostle's commission may include every one of these; yet their work entails more executions, power displays, violent confrontations and so on. A missionary can be decades in a foreign land helping the people without the knowledge of the government in many cases. Unless they stir up trouble by turning the people against their government, no encounter between the two will likely take place, although it must be pointed out that anyone who carries the word of Jesus Christ can unavoidably stir up trouble. Still, with that, the boundaries between the two ministers vary greatly. Sharp limitations are delineated between the two servants that bluntly establish one above the other.

The apostle is sent to aggressively take back what was stolen. To support his mandate of aggression, he is given enormous powers and phenomenal supernatural support. He is sent to deliberately and strategically overturn the status quo; to purposely clash head-on with the powers that be, and to determinedly face off with the foes of darkness guarding the territory. The apostle does not falter into his position but has been indoctrinated by God. He is forewarned and forearmed for the work he must do. He is not naively stumbling into the devil's camp. The apostle doesn't wake up one day wondering how he got to be where he is. The true apostle has had dramatic encounters with the resurrected Christ where the orders, plans, strategies, and assignments that constitute his ministry were delivered to him personally in a one-on-one situation. The supernatural interchange between the apostle and his Lord makes up the very core of the apostolic ministry. The apostle is not a blind zealot, but a fully persuaded, thoroughly indoctrinated messenger of God. (#2)

The apostle's presence in a land or a territory makes a difference. There is no indifferent response to his presence. The apostle's very demeanor exudes an unnerving air that unsettles demonic powers wherever he goes. His appearance in an area awakens the complacent guards of Satan's camps and from the moment he steps into the devil's arena, battle lines are drawn. While humans may not know what makes an apostle an apostle, the demons do. They have historically tangled with the apostolic anointing and this officer and know from experience what is about to take place.

The Apostolic Ministry is never docile; it is never quiet, never easy on the nerves or soothing to the norm. The Apostolic Ministry is catalytic; and count on it, when this move takes place in the earth, once again the world *will* be turned upside down. It is for all these very reasons the devil so hates the apostle. He trembles at the prophet, but he is terrified of the apostle.

Later we will look at some of the overall characteristics of the office and traits of the officer. Right now we are going to answer the controversy over whether or not God has apostles today. Traditional theology says he does not need them. Enlightened research will show otherwise. We are going to explore how many apostles God needs, how often they are needed, what modern apostles do, and how God inducts apostles today. These issues will be discussed separately and briefly. (#3)

Apostololos Is The Old Testament Shaliach

One institution pretypified the apostolate in ancient Israel (and in Hellenism). During her dusk years it flourished under religious societies. Drawn from Semitic, Greek, and Aramaic languages, the institution became the answer to the dispersion's problem of contact and unity. To remedy their problem and to keep their historical and providential destiny alive in the soul of the Diaspora, the leaders sent emissaries to the lands God had scattered the nation to. The country enlisted emissaries dispatched for extended periods of time to collect funds, to revive Judaism, and to increase the converts. They were deputized with the authority of the leaders and given free reign to exercise it in accordance with the purpose, terms and conditions of the commission. The word used for this institution is *Shaliach*. It is the Hebrew counterpart for the Greek word *apostolos*. Both words mean primarily the same things to both groups. The Shaliach lacks an evangelistic and missionary component and stresses legalism more than religious, as it was a mainly secular order.

The Apostolate As A Plenipotentiary

The apostolate, as defined in several sources, is a standing office of a religious institution. The office has full divine accreditation with a universal commission. The position gives its officer full authority to initiate and act on behalf of his institution. He is its subsidiary. The apostolate is designed to revolve around oddly interactive and uniquely participatory exchange between the Lord and the apostle. The office is more than a position or prescribed job description, it is a charge. Here is what the scriptures mean when they refer to having a charge to keep. With the Christian apostle, the Lord stands behind what He says and does. He is the very subject of their message and the essence of their potency.

Every aspect of the apostle's composition and executions may be found in understanding plenipotentiary. His consciousness, his wisdom, his thought processes, and perspectives are all bound up in the significance of this term. The attitude he displays and the emphases of his conscientiousness are all molded to the substance of this word. Since the apostle's commission is mandated, plenipotentiary is the single word that sums up its fullness, and his work and power.

SUGGESTED ASSIGNMENTS

(These correspond with the numbers of the previous text)

1. Identify modem practices and basic sin-ridden conditions that would justify the Acts 26:18 apostolic mission and note them for later group discussion.

2. Draft a one-page profile of present world and church conditions and their indication of the need for the apostle.

3. The apostle's territory is largely spiritual and embodies the human experience (good or bad). Discuss (after compiling) customs, practices, traditions, and doctrines that the apostle's ministry would offend and clash with. Have students attach Scriptures to their responses.

Chapter Four Review

1. The basic definition of an apostle is what, and how does it differ in the church?

2. How can one avoid struggles with envy or insecurity regarding the 5 Fold's preordinations? Why?

3. Give the divine orders of operative principles.

4. Outline God's decision to use an apostle.

5. Explain why and how the apostle is most stringently used. Give Scripture.

6. Discuss the apostolic role in the plan of redemption.

7. Review and discuss the conditions ripe for Apostolic Ministry. Give three present day examples of your own.

8. Illustrate the nine things apostles do.

9.   Why are apostles the fewest in the generations of 5 Fold Ministry?

10.   Define the word "takeover."

11.   Relate #10 to the Church of Jesus Christ.

12.   How is the apostle linked to, and distinct from, the missionary?

13.   Tell the significance of an apostle's being a delegate.

14.   The section on Paul's credibility was intended to accomplish what?

15.   Outline the teaching on the Power of Commission.

16.   Discuss the most significant features of the Apostle's Ministry.

CHAPTER FIVE
Nature and Attributes of the Anointing

Nature and Attributes of the Anointing

Anointing is the supernatural faculty Christ dispenses to all ministers for His work and its immense labors. Gifts and talents say the minister is capable; the anointing makes him or her divinely able. It appoints, anoints, empowers and enhances the minister's natural self for the work of ministry. The anointing supplies the supernatural power that teaches and releases the workers in God's kingdom. It is needed to render their latent ministry gifts and talents "divinely" active. The anointing engages ministers' superior forces, and raises their native endowments to their place of efficacy, readiness, and reliability.

This process may or may not "click" with the minister's historical or experiential abilities. In some instances, it may even attack them. Nevertheless, when the anointing is allowed to excel, it will perform consistently over and above that which the minister normally sees and knows himself to be accustomed to performing. In brief, let it be said that the anointing constitutes the Lord God's ministerial providence at work.

Anointing in this context refers to that divine upgrade, refinement, and empowerment that renders the minister's natural talents usable to God and helpful to His Body. The anointing, being first the Person of Jesus Christ, is also how He flows. However, it is not limited to the Lord's flows only, but is personality driven and reflects His character, His will, His moods, and even His temperament. The anointing is rational, strategic, methodical, purposeful, and deliberative. It includes faculty, resource, capacity, and capability. The anointing also enlarges the person so that the dual existence of them both can cohabit the same vessel with the distinctives of each remaining in tact. It is, in addition, efficacious, dynamic, and power packed.

The anointing is dispensed on two levels: *the gift level and the manifestation level.* It is much like the general effect of the Holy Spirit's presence in our experiential lives. On the gift level, the anointing is a capacitator as well as a supplement. That means it makes you able and makes space to accommodate for what you don't have. The anointing in this effect fuses with your natural talents and perfectly enables them to perform, to produce, and to present themselves to the Holy Spirit as needed. The supplement aspect of the gift level is filling the space created by the Spirit with that which Christ needs you to possess to be ready for His service and assured of success when you are called upon. This includes enlivening the dormant gifts God deposited in you for His ministry use.

On the manifestation level, the anointing exhibits more of its own personality and superiority. The Person of the Godhead becomes more evident. Here is where the Lord's use of the vessel takes over. Where on the first level the *vessel employs* the anointing, on the second and highest level, the *anointing employs* the vessel. At this stage, the vessel is acutely aware of being caught up in what the Lord is using them to do. For one thing, what the vessel ordinarily does well, he now executes exceptionally well. With precision performance, quickness and competence, he is moving at startling speed, carried away with the work of the Lord as he dispenses that which the anointing has brought for those who come to him. As though he is two people at once the servant is aware of his remarkable ability and performance and can almost see himself moving with the Spirit of God, unable to explain why he is doing it or describe how. He simply knows he is upgraded beyond his physical and human self and is more efficient in his service than normal. Beyond that, all he can say is that he cannot duplicate or repeat the act until the Spirit wills.

What the preceding example says to the vessels of God's service is that the minister will ever need the Lord. He will never initiate on his own the performance that he knows is the direct action of the Spirit of God. He will, therefore, ever need the Lord, and the Lord will always see that he will be obliged to rely on Him. Thus their union of service remains effective as God and His Son will continue to be glorified.

Prior to discussing the attributes, a discussion of the anointing, taken from *Constructing the Contemporary Prophet*, follows. It will aid your apprehension of the material that accompanies it. Also, refer to the same text for information on "Dunamis vs. Exousia Power" and "A Study of Miracles."

The Chrio Anointing: The Anointing for Ministry

No word best describes the matchless empowerment God gives people for His service as "the ministerial anointing." Often there is much confusion over the separate enduement God adds to a vessel once He has called him or her into His service. Popular teaching insists there is no difference between what the minister has and what God gives to all His children. At first glance, the argument for evenhanded distributions throughout the Body seems plausible. At the least it is comforting to those whose frail egos cannot fathom one person being more endowed than others. They feel the only reason God would have for making any such difference would be favoritism. You see, man cannot help but see God as unreasonable as he knows himself to be. Consequently, when it comes to the anointing there is much error.

The standard consensus is that whatever God imparts to make us His children is sufficient enough, and comparable with, what we will need to fulfill our ministerial duties. This fact is, frankly, not so. The two dispensations are entirely different in nature, quality, intensity, and density. These differences account for the success of one minister and the crumbling failure of another attempting to imitate him. While God is no respecter of persons, He does regard His handiwork. He may not be impressed with our achievements, but He highly esteems His own. It is on the basis of His own predestiny that God initially gifted one person more than another in one area, and another was made more talented than others in a field. Extending this even further, the variations were made even more pronounced upon conversion. Now the gifted one may no longer be outstanding in that field because what God needs of him is in another area. Meanwhile, the mediocre one is suddenly exceptional in the very field the achiever dominated. Why? The answer is the anointing and the call of God.

For the purpose they were to serve in the world, the natural endowments were sufficient. However, entering God's kingdom, in His eyes, is a promotion. Its labors are weightier and touch a wider sphere of creation. More than the natural, therefore, is needed. The supernatural is called for to enable the minister to not only succeed as always, but to excel as never before. This is accomplished through the anointing we have been talking about.

It is the supernatural outpouring of God upon your vessel for service, called in the Bible, the "baptism of the Holy Spirit." It is for the *enduement*: empowerment or the investment of power, authority, ability, license, and capacity for the work of ministry. This is not, it should be underscored, the same action as that which takes place when one is born again. That is the impartation of the qualities of the Godhead within by the Holy Spirit, upon the Lord's slaughtering your old spirit and implanting the new one in you. To assure you have every opportunity to cease from sin, He adds a measure of Himself inside to guide, strengthen, and quicken you to live and behave as His child. The word used for this action is *chrisma*. It defines the **familial anointing** of God that occurs within upon the new birth. It is what 1 John 2:27 is talking about, and what converts one to the race of the new creation.

What God does on top of that when He equips you for ministry is an additional action. From the **facultative** reservoirs within Himself, instead of the familial ones, God draws strength, fortitude, skill, knowledge and, learning capacity, as well as enrichment for the things He needs his servants to do. Insight, wisdom, awareness, courage, and boldness accompany the ministerial anointing. God's encounter with Moses and Joshua are examples of this. What Christ got when the Dove descended upon Him is what this was talking about.

Being the very Son of God Himself, He certainly did not need to be born again. He was born sinless as the incarnate God. What He received upon baptism (a type of the ceremonial washing required of the priest) was power. The power was for service. He was possessed by the Holy Spirit to execute that which the Father had sent Him to do. The name for this anointing is *chrio*. It is the anointing that **consecrates to service** to furnish what is needed for ministry. The anointing is what is referred to in Acts 1:8 and 10:38.

Chrio properties are heavier, more apparent, and more dominating. Chrio spurs you to act on behalf of God and supplies what you need to do as you need it. Its main distinguishing feature is authority and density. It is more effectual and demonstrates personality, intelligence, purpose, and drive. It is commanding. Anyone who has ever been overtaken by the anointing command of the Holy Spirit to do something can tell you the unmistakable difference between the *chrisma* and the *chrio*.

When the Old Testament prophets spoke of the anointing, it was chrio and not chrisma they were referring to. The new birth was not needed for their external vesting of the Holy Spirit's empowerments; only an ordination by the Lord. On the other hand, what was needed for the indwelling of the Holy Spirit is something else altogether. Here the nature change must be accomplished. Until Christ, the legal ground for God to do this was not yet obtained. So the Old Testament prophets who spoke of being weighed down by the hand of the Lord, or being rendered supernaturally superior, were made so by the chrio anointing. For more information on this subject, read the section on it from the recommended text.

EXERCISE: THE ANOINTING

1.   Give an example of the two levels of anointing.

2.   Cite a gift anointing.

3.   Cite a manifestation anointing.

4.   Outline three features and manifestations of the Ministerial Anointing.

5.   Do the same as #4 for the Familial Anointing.

6.   Give three signs of the Chrisma Anointing's Manifestation.

7.   Give five signs of the Chrio Manifestation.

Apostolic Anointing Attributes

1.   Apostles have a high capacity for envisioning and effectively planning. They are primarily driven by their vision when planning. Since order and structure are important to them, programming and strategizing are key to their activities and are always targeted to bring those visions to pass. A teaching-preaching ministry generates their educational component as member and worker enlightenment is critical to these ministers of the Lord. They simply cannot abide by ignorance to God, His ways, or His righteousness; which they are convinced will be the ruin of their ministry and the downfall of those they have gleaned for Christ. With this understanding deeply etched in their minds, apostles know to condone ignorance is to endorse certain sin; and subsequently, to incur for the believer the chastening of the Lord.

Suggestion: Give your examples of what you understand to be apostolic interpretation, perception, and wisdom from the Book of Acts.

2.   Apostles have a capacity, as a result of their visionary nature, for long-range planning. Predictive insight can give some apostles the wisdom to plan as much as twenty years in advance and to project the needs of the organizations they found. Doing so enables them to prepare beforehand for those needs and to equip followers to execute their plans with reasonable accuracy. Meanwhile, they do not sacrifice short-term impacts in relation to business, government, events, situations, and behavior to assure the future of the organization. For the astute and stable apostle, organization perpetuity is paramount. You will often hear him or her talk about how to keep the works going, thriving, and successful after his or her death. With these tools God uses the mature apostle to establish sound policies, regulations, rules, and other instruments of government. An innate apostolic judicial nature helps to assure formulation of leadership implements is balanced, righteous, godly, life promoting, and geared toward holiness.

3.   Apostolic service to the Lord has a strong developmental and disciplinarian bent. They are superior at confrontations, and skillful in defending their faith, their Savior's mission, and the Father's dreams for mankind. Apostles are relentless in their resolve to make ready a people prepared for the Lord. They do not hesitate to correct and rebuke, but if they have learned well from the Savior, they are sure to follow up stern reactions with warm, reassuring affirmations so as not to alienate corrected sheep from the flock, or to give place for the enemy to brow beat and harass the erring disciple. Nevertheless, the apostle's first line of defense against the contamination of his flock is to confront the sinning one, warn the others, and seek to remediate the wayward soul back to the ways of the Lord.

4.   Apostle's have commendable teaching and evaluative skills and piercing discernment. We have discussed this at length elsewhere; however, its importance to the apostolic ministry makes it necessary reiteration. In addition, their intuitive instincts are reliable and intense. When it comes to educating their ministers and members, they are adept at spotting learning deficiencies, identifying comprehension barriers and other learning hindrances, and are quick to use the innovative gifts God has given them to creatively overcome many of these obstacles in those they teach. Furthermore, the discernment they are endowed with helps them understand the processing faculties of their students so they can vary the delivery methods to meet the individual needs and levels of their learners. Apostles tend to be straightforward about problem resolution and are quick to change techniques, if they understand how, to implement improvement steps that will strengthen the effects of their efforts; and improve the reception of those they minister to.

5.	Apostles, for obvious reasons, possess superior prophetic abilities. They are able to accurately speak the present utterances of God, as well as communicate the revealed intents, desire, will, and plans of God from Scripture. This ability is derived from the remarkable interactions with God they enjoy on an almost continual basis. Such interactions provide for them an open window to the Lord's mind and kingdom, and to the activities of the powers of darkness. Equally powerful interpretive skills mean they can rightly divide what they see and/or perceive by the Spirit. Competent application ability makes them able to relay the Lord's desire for those they serve, and reconcile quite adroitly the will and word of the Lord for those to whom they minister. One thing that will make an apostle continually respected and sought after is his practical wisdom and balanced grasp of the mind of the Lord. When those they counsel hear revelation accompanied by instruction, direction, and insight sharpened by relevance, they are impressed by the well-rounded knowledge they receive. This tends towards trust in the apostle's leadership because of the unusual fruits their ministries bear in the kingdom of God. If the apostle is solidly trained and submitted to the character of the Lord Jesus Christ, the soundness of his doctrine and consultations will draw innumerable souls to his ministry.

6.	Noteworthy of the apostle is his inordinate understanding of leadership, organization, and government. A chief sign of the apostolic mantle is the competent exercise of these qualities. Even the slightly educated minister is impressive when it comes to ordering his ministry. While limited education may prove a hindrance to his potential, his glowing apostolic aptitudes, nevertheless, shine through. Referring back to the fundamental requirement of an apostolic call, founding, grounding and restoration; the demand for organization; policymaking, government, legislative, leadership, and kingdom enforcement skills are a given. The real apostle will possess these rare abilities and astound many with the ability to tackle massive institutional requisites with ease. Of all the offices, these skills are most prevalent and concentrated in the Apostolic Office. Remember, theirs is usually an original work; therefore, the need for these gifts calls for them to be able to, from A to Z, build, structure, organize, and govern the work God gives them to do. For this reason the abilities are strongest in this office. On the other hand, their restoration faculties are gleaning as well. With crystal insight, these peer through organization and operational muddle to swiftly identify problems and their root. Aptly, they sum up needs and uncover solutions to help put wandering institutions back on God's track.

7.	Apostles are missions and outreach minded and have global emphases to their work. Also, realizing that theirs is a work of duration, their efforts center on the here and now, as well as the hereafter.	If a person is a bona fide apostle, then he will have a vibrant, true apprehension of the hereafter. Many of them have been told by the Lord, like Peter in John's Gospel, and Paul in the Book of the Philippians, how long (in non-specific terms) their work will last and what the eternal future holds for them. They have seen Christ in His Kingdom and eagerly await the commencement of His reign. Tasty bites of His glory have been shared with them and they have no hesitancy about wrapping up their work and getting on with the hereafter. For them, visions of paradise, even though many of them protect these for prudent reasons, are not uncommon.

8.	God's good pleasure is the chief motivation of their service. Apostles, undoubtedly, have gone through painful separation processes before being trusted with their mission. The disentanglements are strenuous and taxing on their inner self. Most are bruised inside from the events that led to, and culminated in, their call. You will recall that separation is the crux of their extraction from the world. It is what constitutes their usefulness to the Lord. Alienation and isolation from the masses propels them to the comfort and friendship of the Lord. They seek solace from the despairs that surround their ministry in the heart and soul of the Lord. Eventually after severing numerous ties, they ultimately resort to Him for all their needs. As it happens, this was the goal of the Lord all the time, since the drastic upheavals of the call and its rigorous demands create the need for the apostle to be ever drawn into conferences and snap meetings with the Christ. The result of these meetings further add to the isolation as the knowledge they walk away with severs more the relations they may have in the world. It is the sum of these that drive the apostle into the heart of the Father and the womb of the Holy Spirit. Upon finding his place and space in the Godhead, he soon recovers to make Christ his all in all, and centralize Him as the chief reason for his being and his ministry.

9.   Apostles, for all the reasons given above, possess a deep affection for the Lord. It ends up being the single impetus behind their slavish devotion to Him and their work. The apostolic anointing will have, as a result, exceptional experiences with the Lord outside of duty commands and ministry requirements. A genuine flame of friendship, camaraderie, and fellowship exists between the two. Whatever field of the Lord's Being the apostle is assigned to, he from that perspective, develops into a confidant and even comforter of the Lord. Thus, their experiences, though private, are transformative, giving the apostle the final push he needs to settle down with his Christ relationship and forget those things which are behind. Even though you would be hard pressed to get into the deep excursions apostles have with the Lord, you can witness the fruit of them as they carry on the work Jesus gave them to do.

10.   Power—latent, dormant, overt, and dynamic—characterize the execution of the office. Nothing is more staggering, or more boggling to the mind than to witness apostolic power in action. The gravity of their mandate and the charge of the Lord upon them require exemplary power to facilitate the discharge of their duties. Fierce confrontations and opposition, beyond this, make the need for uncustomary power even more pressing. The scope of their ministry, their degree of supernatural contact, all explain the merits of their broad power and authority base.

Suggestion: Using Moses and Paul as examples, cite three Bible accounts of the above.

11.   Authority is the main feature of credibility for the office. It is the convincing factor that announces this is not your everyday run-of-the-mill preacher. Apostles command respect and capture the attention of even the most indifferent observer with their skillful articulation of the word of the Lord. Their revelations are stirring and tend to overwhelm those who hear them for a variety of reasons. Authority to judge, to act, to initiate, to install, to institute, and to govern is integral to the mission and its mandate. Apostles must be heard; they must be allowed access to the hearts and souls of the people of God. They must have ample outlets in the way God is moving, and they must receive every opportunity to sway the flock the way God wants. His mission is to reposition the kingdom as Christ dictates. Whatever it takes to see that the apostle gets through, that his message gets delivered, and that what he is sent to overturn, restore, and establish occurs in its season, God will pull out all stops to do. Apostles also have, to expedite their business, great strategic and tactical senses.

Suggestion: Using Acts and Corinthians, find two examples of #11.

12.   The nature of the office is *judicial* (not judgmental as many would like to contend), executive, and administrative. It is also spiritual, and biblical responsibilities identify it. Apostles are more than dual-strata officers, they are multi-strata. Their secular training often gives them roots in the world for its evangelism. The divine mandate equips them for spiritual, eternal, supernatural and demonic interactions. Hence, their actions in this world cannot help but spill over to address the myriad of influences that affect the church they are to defend, keep, nurture, multiply, and vice versa. In addition to their repositioning mandate, the apostle knows he is duty-bound to present the Bride blameless to Christ.

Suggestion: Describe and illustrate the apostle's dual and multi-strata roles.

Chapter Five Review 1

1. Compare the apostle's visionary insight with his inclination toward education.

2. Discuss the apostle's insightful planning abilities.

3. Development and discipline are central to the apostle's service. How and why?

4. The apostle's abilities in relation to teaching and learning consist of what? Give an example.

5. Describe the apostle's prophetic abilities.

6. Explain the apostle's superior leadership styles.

7. Tell why missions and outreach are vital to the apostle.

8. Review the apostle's separation process.

9. Comment on the apostle's deep affection for the Lord and its influences.

10. Describe the power that characterizes the apostle's office.

11. Name the feature credibility of the office and discuss it.

12. Shed light on the office's judicial nature.

Apostolic Foundations

In this section, you will learn not only the elements of the apostle's office, but you will understand how deliberate Jesus' appointment of him as the founder and establisher of His church was. Research will show that the Lord's choice of terms was calculated and meant to inject a staggering force of ability into the kingdom of God. To help you appreciate the breadth of understanding you are about to receive, a comparison is in order. Explaining how God arrived at His appropriation of the term and what it aimed to convey to the people of that day will go a long way to open your mind to what is to come.

If you were to go back to the time when the Lord brought Israel out of Egypt you would appreciate how He instituted the Levitical Priesthood. God ordained the offerings, the sacrifices, and the rites of observance for their practice. He established who would be the servants (temple ministers) and who would deliver up the sacrifices (the priests). The lineage of Aaron was chosen for the priestly functions, and one of them would be appointed high priest. As you read this account you notice that not once did the people seek an explanation of what a priest was. No one interrupted Moses' discourse, asking, "What is a priest, and what is a *high* priest?" Somehow the people knew exactly what the Lord was saying and were able to follow Moses completely as he outlined the demands of Jehovah.

In the book of Leviticus, the reason for this becomes clear. Turn to chapter seventeen and it will become clear to you as well; specifically 17:1-9. You will see that the tone of God's discussion implies the people were already sacrificing animals and were quite accustomed to a priesthood.   History will prove that a class of priests go as far back as Abraham and even before then. In fact, Jethro, Moses' father-in-law, was a priest of Midian when the Aaronic Priesthood had yet to be established. He was evidently accepted by Moses during the forty years he spent with the man and his family as one of a priestly class. Actually, you could say that Moses' experience with Jethro added to his being able to establish the kingdom designed by Jehovah once Israel was freed from Egyptian bondage. Jethro's priestly functions were no doubt known to Moses who had probably witnessed them for years, making his Mount Sinai conversations with the Lord much easier to take in. This coupled with Moses' life in Pharaoh's house made the concept of priestly officiations quite commonplace. So by the time he had to deliver the worship demands of the Lord to the people, Moses was knowledgeable of what he was saying.

Moreover, the people's captivity experience well-oriented them to the customs and practices of worship and ritual sacrifices. The idea—better yet, the compulsion—to sacrifice slaughtered animals was ingrained in them. It was the *object* of their sacrifice the Lord took issue with. Instead of to demons, as Leviticus 17:7 puts it, the people were now to redirect their offerings to the Lord God Jehovah, who delivered them out of the house of bondage. Instead of killing innocent animals for just any old reason, they were now to do so to commemorate and show gratitude for their salvation to honor their covenant with God Most High.

Down through the years, the Scriptures show us how God permits man to become familiar with his own idea of something, and once that knowledge becomes familiar to him, the Lord takes the concept and places it in His own program. The same is true with Christ's selection of the term **apostle**. Researching the word's meaning indicates that apostles as a professional order in the empire's service were not foreign to the people of His day. They did not stumble at the idea of the Lord instituting His own order of apostles. Peter and the others seemed quite comfortable with it. More than that, they relished it. They were apostles of the Lord Jesus Christ. To them that meant something—something awesome. So clear were they on the matter, that Peter was taken aback by Christ's revelation of His impending crucifixion (See Luke 22:31). Peter could not fathom it because his understanding of what they were and what they were doing as the Lord's apostles was to take the kingdom back from the Romans. (Look at Peter's confusion in Matthews 16:21-23). It took the Pentecost Baptism to show them otherwise. Until then, the idea of Jesus' death was beyond them.

The role of an apostle, as their culture understood it, was to take back what was stolen or illegally seized and to restore it to its rightful owner. (See their attitude as revealed in Acts 1:6. The apostle of their day also established conquered territories in the ways and will of the new king. They were apostles and though Jesus had died, He had returned to them). Surely now they would finish their mission and fulfill their purpose. Now they would do what apostles before them had done. They would usher in change, overturn the enemy's strongholds, free the captives, and take back the nation for God. Certainly now Israel was to again be a free nation. After all, that is what apostles do, don't they?

Ah, but Jesus had greater plans in mind. He was not looking to restore Israel only, but to regain the world of humanity for His Father. He was not looking to overturn the Roman Empire, but to overturn Satan's. He was not sent to apostle a nation, but the entire world. His mission was not to save Israel from the Romans but the world from sin. His commission was to establish the kingdom of God on earth. Yes, He was the apostle of a new move, but it was an unprecedented one. He was the apostle of the "called out ones." His mandate was the accomplishment of Daniel 7:13,14 and the fulfillment of Genesis 3:15.

As the first Apostle of the new covenant, Christ was to bring many sons and daughters to God and to set the stage for the final curtain of Satan's reign. He would take back the kingdoms of this world for the Lord God Almighty; in much the same way the earthly apostles were taking kingdoms for their king. Oh, it was so plain to the apostles, they thought. Luke 19:11 shows how they saw the commission and the mission. It was radically different from what Christ was sent to do. Therefore, He had to correct them, and look at the parable He uses to do it.

It is about a nobleman who is to inherit a kingdom one day. The kingdom is illegally seized and run by cruel leaders who hate the king. They did not want him to reign over them so they chose their own leaders. After a while the nobleman, who was sent away on a long journey, returned to settle accounts with those he left in charge. The last verse, Luke 11:27, says it all: The man received his kingdom; his faithful servants took care of his business and were rewarded; the evil revolutionaries lost their battle and were punished by the newly appointed king, who disposed of them for their crimes.

The apostles' well understood the parable and were astonished to learn that all that Jesus did was for a spiritual struggle, and the restoration of the kingdom they expected would be only in the invisible realm. They found it disheartening to discover the restorations of the natural orders were coming much later in God's program. Yet the notion of an apostolic ministry, you can see from all this, was not foreign to them. Here is why.

Jesus used the word almost casually, and research uncovers the term **apostle** was not a new one. At least, it is employed as though it was well understood in Christ's day. Much like, for example, the word crucifixion.

Exploring the root of the word *apostle* shows it goes all the way back before the Greek empire, as its etymology is found in their language. Based on this, it may be, the Roman Empire's aggressive campaign of conquering nations and enlarging its territory created the need to explore their Greek influences to find a word to define the commissions they were handing out. A single term was needed to classify those they sent as ambassadors of the kingdom and generals of the king's best interests. Research, in response to this, uncovered the term *apostle* was appropriate. It was to be used in much the same way as the Greeks used it: to identify an order of high ranking ambassadors with military might, powers of persuasion and diplomacy, and the ability to disciple captives and converts to the culture and laws of their kingdom.

It would seem that these diplomatic generals were accorded enormous powers and comprised an elite commission to propagate the aims of the empire and unify its citizenry. In addition, they were to, forcefully if need be, enlarge the king's territory and stabilize its holdings. The core of these emissaries' authority, it appears, included overthrow, legislative license, judicial power, and governmental jurisdictions. They evidently constituted the chief rulers of the region they apostled, influential leaders driven to induce converts to become settled and productive in the kingdom.

Research of key terms used to define apostle and their customary usage further unfolds the apostles were, in addition to being generals, strategists and territorial warriors. They were purpose oriented, focused, and committed to the king's service. Their allegiance to him appears to be unfailing and undying. Their word was as fierce as their actions and became law to demonstrate the powers and authorities they possessed. Lastly, for obvious reasons, diplomacy being chief among them, these superior agents of the king's service were highly educated and intelligent. The ability to communicate the mind of the king,, his will, thoughts and ways to those brought into the kingdom called for excellence in speech and other forms of communications. Therefore, these apostles were highly trained and extremely knowledgeable.

Education, as is the case with any takeover or takeback, is key to the orientation of any newly organized or restructured entity. Hence, catechism figures prominently in apostleship. Once a group has been conquered and inducted into the mainstream, the next most prudent step is to catechize them. The word catechism, which we have come to associate strictly with the Catholic religion, has many meanings. It does have its roots in religion, but much of its object has to do with socializing. Catechism covers systemization, indoctrination, teaching, interrogation and, apostolizing. It defines education, illumination, civilizing, guidance, enlightenment, and instruction. The word's use is expanded to include formulation of beliefs, principles of doctrine and dogma, articles of faith, and philosophical creeds. For all these reasons, the apostle's mandate demands education and orientation.

Whether in the church or in another culture, the elementary principles of the knowledge and wisdom of the land must be learned if the new additions to the kingdom are to become skilled in them and made socially productive functional citizens of society. Consequently, the capacities of the apostle are enhanced by strong articulation abilities. Those appointed would need as their highest gift the ability to make the deep, mysterious, and obscure plain and easy to understand. Doing so enables them to expedite newcomer adaptation to the culture of the kingdom, and to nurture a body of responsible converts to the orders and regimes of the king.

Institution building and development, and the cultivation of educators to develop and stabilize the new converts, is innate to the apostolate. The ability to draft a systematic means of laying forth, verbally, relative foundational teachings emerges as one of the mandates of its call by definition. This definition explains the basis for the need of the commissioned ones to communicate ground level knowledge to those in their care.

What makes these revelations highly probable of the apostle's mantle is the writers' of the New Testament ease of application of the term, and their profound expositions on the officer's duties. When Jesus called His disciples and renamed them apostles, a basic apprehension of what the title meant and how it was applied is conveyed in the writings. The disciples seemingly grasped fully the connotations of the distinctions Jesus made between themselves and the others. Later in the book of Acts, the officials' reaction to the mission and activities of the twelve indicate they too comprehended the nature and scope of what they were doing. The impact of the apostles' authority was very real to them. The attachment of the name of Jesus to what they were doing further antagonized and terrified them. Throughout the New Testament, references to the word *apostle* are made with the assumption that its meaning was well understood by those who heard it. Paul's teachings on the subject further underscore this statement in that it is presented as though the concept of the apostle in general need not be elaborated on; only his function in the Body of Christ.

The explanations that follow will give insight into why Paul treated it that way. The word *apostle* comes from many Greek variants. Studying their use and definitions, tracing the numerous references and allusions, provides us with a body of meaningful implications surrounding the word; implications that pretty much settle the definitive questions regarding the office, its intent, powers, purpose, and use by God. Analyses of all the terms and references so enlarges its meanings and applications that the unveiling of the office and its operations is achieved. Through them, the divine design is made known and the premise we have been discussing is confirmed. Now for the etymology of the word.

Apostle: The Meaning of the Word

The prefix **-apo** is where we will begin. It means "away from." It describes a complete separation. *Apo* infers a consecration from the masses to fulfill a commission. The word *apostle* itself comes from the Greek *apostello*. It means "set apart to send out on a mission by being liberated from previous obligations." In the strictest sense, Ezra and Nehemiah, under King Cyrus, are good examples of this. They were both occupying other positions. Yet when the king was inspired by the Lord to restore Judaism, they were formally relieved of their duties to set out on the commission he ordained.

You can easily see the connection between the prefix and the word *apostle*. From here we were led to the word *apostle*. It enriches our understanding further by adding to our meanings, **"a commission, an apostolate, an apostleship."** To build further on our definition, we uncovered the Greek word *apostolos*. Our original meaning is now enlarged to include the definition, "a delegate; an ambassador of the Gospel; Christ's commissioner; an apostle; one with miraculous powers; a sent messenger."

Apo, which we defined above, plus *stello* is what gives us our word apostle. Together, they tell us what the office and its officer is, does, and is required to do. *Stello* means, in addition, "strengthened, set fast." It implies as well, "a withdrawal that precludes customary associations with." Its use comes from roots that mean, *"a standing appointment established by covenant."*

Apostles, like all the five-fold, are a set aside group, ordained for the purpose of setting forth the new covenant kingdom of Jesus Christ. What makes this study even more interesting is the discovery of the apostolic ministry's link to military leadership and might. It is what brought us to the conclusion that is the subject of this section.

It was both startling and amazing to find the officer's mantle included warfare, strategy and rulership. According to the terms that make reference to the apostolate, they go hand in hand with the officer's other mandates. Related Greek terms reveal the strategy aspect of the ministry. One particular term— which tracing the *apostolate* led to—stands out. Its meaning makes a direct reference to the apostleship. The word **strateia**, defining a military service, it says is as an apostolic career. The word's intent is amplified by a kin term, *strateuomai*, whose meaning is "to serve in a military campaign; to execute the apostolate with its arduous duties and functions; contending with carnal inclinations." This word's definition speaks of armaments, troops, and battle array. The idea encompasses a general with governorship authority that spills over into priestly and religious affairs. It addresses even temple care and guardianship.

The apostle surfaces through these meanings as an arch warrior, a chief strategist, a competent captain, and an able guard over his jurisdiction. His catechism mandate, covered extensively elsewhere, means he is an apt teacher and thus highly intelligent. His supernatural rank in the stratos makes him a formidable combatant in the spirit realm and an arch rival to the forces in the heavenlies. His divine commission establishes him as a conscientious, dutiful priest of the New Covenant under the High Priestly office of Jesus Christ.

The apostle's realm covers, spiritually and supernaturally, religion, military, government, and education, as they pertain to realms of God's creation. From this it is clear that the concepts of apostolic power and authority were not foreign to the people of Jesus' day and its transference to the exclusive use of Christ the Savior was strategically intended.

All this is to say that apostles existed and were used in the secular world and are commonly accepted agents of a new move. This view bears out our opening remarks, stating that apostles are peculiarly suited to new moves. In the church of Jesus, they are integral to the new moves of God. The book of Acts (5:35-39) shows this position was held by the Jewish Leaders.

The use of the word goes back to the Greek language and must have found its place in the culture of that kingdom. The word thus existed prior to the Christ's incarnation. The attention given it, its position of apparent rank in the government, the military, and the mind of the citizens reflects its accepted poli-religious place in the empire. The apostolate, to conclude, can be broken down into distinct areas:

Commission - Religion - Military - Government - Education – Ambassadorship

Chapter Five Review 2

1. What made Jesus' use of the word *apostle* calculated, and what did it inject in God's kingdom?

2. Discuss the foundation laid for the teaching.

3. What was the implied scope of the officer based on the application of the term?

4. Explain the role of Catechism in the Apostle's Ministry.

5. Why must the apostle's faculties be enhanced by strong articulation abilities?

6. Discuss what the New Testament writers understood from Jesus' invocation of the term.

7. Cover the nine elements of the apostle's order, rank, duty, and authority.

Apostolic Ministry/Mantle Features

1. *Sent Forth*

    This refers to the dispatching of the apostle to the besieged dungeons of the world to free those imprisoned to the devil through the flesh. It is an imperative mark of the office. While we have proven that a mission does not make the apostle, an apostle without a mission is also not possible. The mission is the object and outcome of the burning flames of devotion and indignation that spark apostolic fervor. His electric personality set wholly in the soul of Jesus Christ would stagnate if he were to be a pew warmer or confined to a church-only ministry. An apostle is a world class minister whose field is the world and whose territory is all the kingdom of God's and Satan's. Without a goal oriented mission, the apostle cannot be "a sent one," he is merely "a called out one." The distinction is pointedly made in Luke 9:1-5 and clarified in Matthew I0:1-42.

2. *Strong Missionary Component*

    A strong missionary component is fundamental to the office as a result of the basic definition of its call. Since enough attention has been given to this subject elsewhere, it will not be expounded on further here. See earlier address of this discussion in the beginning of this section and compare it to the statements made in number one above.

3. *A Catalyst*

    The apostle is a catalyst for all the other offices to follow. No single word best captures the effect of the apostle than **catalyst** By definition, the word contains the full scope and impact of their ministry. A catalyst, chemically speaking, is an agent that ignites the reactions of others. It is a reaction mechanism that instigates change, alteration, or transformation. Instigation is one of the three major affects of a catalyst. The others are cause and transformation. Together, they convey the forceful impact apostles make on the planet.

    Apostolic mantles are causative forces, in contrast to the prophet who is detonating. The apostle causes the fire that sets in motion the change of events and circumstances that completely disrupts the status quo. He is inflammatory, provocative, agitating and inciteful. Paul's charges from the Ephesians and other nations he traveled to was that he incited uproars among the crowds wherever he went.

    Apostles' relentless drive to manifest God's truth and the Son of God makes them irritating and discomforting to those hiding out from the Lord. Their innovative approaches to doing the work of ministry to reach and persuade many is an impressive mark of their sweeping abilities. Transformations occur wherever they go and tend to dominate their movements. One could hardly be in the presence of the apostle and remain unaffected by the anointing. Encounters with apostles are stirring, bringing about deep, moving, and often agonizing life-altering experiences.

    The apostle's ministry arises out of a dramatic call, conversion, and dispatch. His call has much to do with the apostolic fervor and commitment he is known for. The question of genuine call, a specific dispatch, and a definite empowerment and purpose are forever settled in the memory of his stinging confrontation with the Savior. The apostle is not summoned by a gentle tug felt during an especially high church service. The apostle is, for the most part, knocked off his feet and dragged to the altar of God. Apostles are ordinarily headstrong people happily on their own course of life, doing what they want to do when they want to do it. Independence is a forceful influence in their lives until they are met by Christ, who powerfully enlists them to do His will. It is not uncommon for more than a few apostles to confide, having tangled with the Lord on several occasions as He proved to them Who He is and what they are in comparison. Many recall jolting object lessons as part of their early training sessions. Some even have lasting scars (visibly or inwardly) to remind them the Lord is not to be toyed with.

Apostolic obedience, for this reason, is disturbing to most saints. It acts like a spotlight glaring down on their casual submission to Christ. Years of grooming and pruning went into bringing the apostle to his knees before getting him into God's purpose. Whatever portion of the Lord's message he receives, the apostle's excruciating preparation has taught him well to deliver thoroughly and accurately all that the Savior has put in his mouth and his soul.

Suggestion: Give three examples of behaviors that would indicate this attitude.

4. *Founder and Grounder*

   Always a founder and groundbreaker, the apostle is a pioneer sent to dry, hard, barren ground. He is, moreover, the ice breaker. The nature of the office demands this condition of service. The apostle is always the one who is sent, or raised up, to break petrified religious and spiritual ground. He is sent to renew, to reestablish, to restore, and redirect and return the people of God to Him. The apostle is needed when the moorings of apostasy, pseudo religion, and cosmopolitanism have all subverted the church. His work is on many planes. He is the founder or grounder of the sincere religious establishment. He is the restorer of the true faith in Jesus Christ. He redirects believers' focus back to the real Redeemer. He returns the lost, slaughtered, and scattered, bewildered sheep of Christ back to the fold of God. Apostolic fire ignites renewed worship, inspires heartfelt praise, and fuels godly devotion and commitment. It crumbles sin and reestablishes holiness and righteousness in God's kingdom.

   Suggestion: From your experience and observation, come up with a composite that reflects the above condition in existence.

5. *Load Bearer*

   This may seem like an odd phrase to include in our analysis, but it is an intense responsibility that accompanies the work. Of all the officers, the apostle's load is the heaviest, and here is why. The prophet is itinerant, but may not have a church and thus is free from pastoral responsibility. It is not advisable that seasoned prophets even maintain a church, as the conflicts between the two anointings, can clash and subject one to the other. The pastor, to continue, has a church, but is ideally not itinerant. There are no New Testament examples of itinerant pastors, and for good reason. The nature of the office demands the flock not be left unattended or abandoned. The mission of the apostle is to restore, not contribute to, scattered or abandoned sheep. He is their solution, not their problem's cause. It is hazardous to the sheep's well being to be left in the care of hirelings. Hirelings are those engaged to baby-sit the church in the pastor's absence. Because they have neither birthed nor carried the sheep in their bosom, their care is often not the same. They are not the owners of the sheep, but the attendants. Extended use of them can corrupt or contaminate the flock, not to mention the potential of displacing the pastor as their shepherd in their eyes.

To continue our comparisons, the teacher has classroom responsibility and typically does not have to be consumed with the edification of a congregation. He also is scarcely itinerant. The evangelist is a field worker without nurturing responsibility. Essentially he preaches and leaves, turning over the new converts to the shepherds to disciple and care for. The apostle alone must bear the load of covering, in all aspects, the entire range of ministerial functions for the Body of Christ brought into or birthed by his movement.

In contrast to the others, the apostle's load is heavier for these reasons. He must carry the weight of all the others until he has birthed, trained, and raised up the five-folders of his mission's movement. To these, we can add the other duties characteristic of the office itself. The apostle must evangelize, prophesy, pastor and teach. His founding work means his duties are expanded to include policymaking, organizing, executive management, and administration. Government and staff preparation and development are to be part of his workload as well. The apostle as a founder and designer of the organization he builds will formulate the plans, policies, and practices that carry on his ministry and its operations. The apostle's world field mission makes him party to much of the secular events that necessitate his ministry; besides his ecclesiastical and managerial duties. Therefore, he is most certain to be pulled into the behind the scenes activities of society as an advisor, intercessor, and officiate of normal human affairs.

Suggestion: Outline, based on above, the typical apostle's ministry program.

6. *Discretionary Power and Authority*

The office has, for the reasons laid down in prior examinations of the title, unrestricted discretionary use of God's power. The operative word here is discretionary. It means free will, unbridled, independent, elective and spontaneous. The delegate and commissarial aspects of the call mean the apostle is a distant operative of the king. Therefore, the prospects of remotely managing him are slim. He is either faithful or not. The training and preparation given him for his ministry are effective or they are not. Either way, the apostle is mostly on his own and has to be trusted to exercise his delegation and to discharge his duties as he sees fit. To get a better picture of this, refer back to the Apostolic Foundations. The rebukes and admonishments used to chasten the apostle, however, are the most severe. His authority is derived from the Lord Jesus Christ, even if he is a subordinate apostle. Hence, his strokes for misconduct and misbehavior are sharpest. They need to overwhelm the superior enhancements of ruggedness performed by God to fortify him and strengthen his being. Therefore, though faithful apostles are rarely chastened, when they are it is usually grave and tends to leave a lasting reminder burning in the apostle's memory.

7. *Inherent Power Office*

Of all five, this one is the Inherent Power Office. Based on the explanations from the Apostolic Foundations, the logical reasons for this should be clear. Due to the greatness of the apostle's responsibility and the burden placed upon him to stand in his office, a natural intrinsic power to perform, order, authorize, and govern as well as defend the work is weaved into the very fabric of the Apostle's being. Have you ever wondered what Paul meant when he spoke of his authority and power? Notice how he spoke with such confidence about turning this one over to Satan, or using sharpness that could destroy if he handled it cruelly (2 Corinthians). It is because of the enormous power Christ committed to his trust. It is discretionary power, which is why he could command darkness on a wicked soul, or effectively cut a wayward rebel off from the flock. All the Apostles knew this. Why even Peter pronounced blindness on Simon who tried to bribe him into passing on his gifts for money. And you remember Ananias and Sapphira. The Apostle's rebuke and conviction of them was so potent that it caused them to give up the ghost and die. In all these instances the accuracy of the Apostle's judgment remained unchallenged by the Lord. God expressly attested to their authority by performing whatever word they pronounced. It was their call and discretion, and they made it as they saw fit; the wisdom of the Lord, and the effectual working of the Holy Spirit within them notwithstanding. Hence, the apostle's words emit the power of performance.

8. *Highly Demonstrative*

The apostolate is a highly demonstrative position. It is replete with signs, wonders, and miracles. Demonstration of the Spirit bathe the ministry in the supernatural. Only a chosen few can be entrusted with such power and authority. God does not release this degree of independent action and free will, access to, and use of His authority to any other office. Even the prophet, who can impressively move in the powers of God, cannot wield the degree of power and authority an Apostle does. Why? Because the post requires years of rigorous testing, training, trials, and the like to establish the main criteria for its fulfillment: obedience, loyalty, and devotion. All make up the substance of this calling's standards. Not everyone is willing to suffer, pay the price, or submit to the intense training and scrutiny under the Lord to attain to it. God knew this in advance, so He dispensed the calling to a select few (proportionately speaking) from each generation.

Out of necessity, the Apostle moves in and out of the remaining four offices as we have stressed. He does so in much the same way as Moses, David and Christ stood in the three main offices of their covenant's dispensation: Prophet, Priest and King. Their bestowal of independent actions joined with their monumental tasks of service stipulated broad latitude be given them in service.

Chapter Five Review 3

1.   State the imperative mark of the apostle.

2.   What precludes an apostle being a classic sent one?

3.   Based on the definition of the call, what is the basic fundamental of the office?

4.   Explain the apostle as a catalyst.

5.   Explain the sweeping impact of the apostle's ministry.

6.   Give the basis for and nature of the apostle's call.

7.   Address the details of the apostle's excruciating preparation.

8.   Overview the substantives of the apostle as a pioneer.

9. Review the apostle's founder/grounder activities. Include the dynamics his ministry sparks in the process.

10. Summarize the section on the apostle as a load bearer.

11. Explain the premise for the apostle's discretionary power and authority.

12 What necessitates the apostolate's being an inherent Power Office? Why is it needed?

13. The high demonstrations of the apostle's office are needed and regulated by what? For what reasons? Be specific.

14. How the apostle moves in and out of the remaining four offices was likened to what?

15. For what reasons does he need the latitude to do #14?

The Apostolic Personality

When talking about personality, especially as it relates to or differs from attributes, the distinction between the two has to do with the substantive parts of one's condition or state of life (personality) over their basic nature (the attribute). Attributes constitute a substantial part of a thing's or person's nature and are identified through responses and reactions rather than behaviors and conduct. God, for example, is holy. Holiness is a difficult to locate and pin down trait. However, when confronted with sin, the Lord's natural reflex is to recoil and condemn it. His holiness is offended by the presence of sin and is injured by sinful acts. They are painful, harmful, unpleasant and discomforting to Him for many reasons. The action of sin brings about His reaction to the offense.

Personality is different in that it is the body of expressed perceptions that identify us individually for *who* we are as distinguished from *what* we are. The personality is what divides us and sets us apart from the rest of humanity. Our personality is understood and explained silently through our actions (behaviors, choices, and conduct). The consistent way we handle a situation or approach life is determined by our perceived selfhood. Outlooks, temperament, and mental state are all the product of our personality. A personality, being behavior based, can be changed or modified. An attribute, on the other hand, is fixed in the nature and cannot be altered without a complete destruction and reconstruction of the person. If the attribute says what we are, then the personality says who we are, and how we may be identified and recognized without ever uttering a word. A personality can be, and often is, shaped and molded by a number of influences. It can even effectively hide the true self by restraining certain things and playing up what is believed more favorable for expedient reasons. The same cannot be said for the attributes, which cannot be varied by volition. Discipline may delay the basic human responses, but eventually they will overflow to reveal the nature.

The relationship of this information to the five-fold offices we have been discussing is the basic substance of the offices as rendered active by those who stand in them, and the expressions that identify the officer in contrast to the office he claims. As we go through this information, you may see one statement may emphasize the point the other way around. The intent is to expose you to the features of the office and the officers separately for you to make value judgments concerning the candidates and their operations from informed standpoints, and not from emotionally charged preferences.

From the material so far, you can conclude yourself what apostles are like. To begin with, they are energetic, diligent, and persevering. They are fiercely loyal and defensive of their mission and its work, because for them, it is mandate driven. The following lists other traits of the apostle:

1.   Since apostles are undaunted by the sacrifice and denial, even slave-like demands of the Lord, they are devoted, dedicated and dutiful. They are finishers and tend to despise the habit many Christians have of starting something and because of the work and commitment involved, abandoning the project midstream saying the Lord changed His mind and gave them another assignment to start and not finish. The true

apostle makes a big deal out of completion and bears down heavy upon those who labor with him to cultivate a zeal for finishing what they start. Follow through and follow up are two standards they deem important to credibility and respectability. Some who join forces with the apostolic personality will find this quirk irritating; however, since the greater part of the Body of Christ is made up of those whose histories have been to circumvent order, achievement, and commitment, the need for this particular apostolic emphases cannot be overstated. If an informal poll were taken Body wide, the number of saints who boast of having made it in spite of having not finished high school, not having extended their education beyond high school, or having beat the system would be astounding. Not only is their boast in their educational deprivation, but their underlying mission—their secret mission—becomes to reward others for doing the same. These ministers seek out people who did it the way they did and hand over the reigns of God's kingdom to them to prove a point. Herein lies the explanation for the frustration many congregants feel at the disorganized way their churches are run and the limited capacities of their ministers. The Lord Jesus Himself declared a disciple is not above his teacher. One of the things He meant by this is that the disciple's growth is determined by those he submits himself to learn from. A twelfth grade education not augmented by extensive, challenging, and vigorous self-study or post secondary seminars, etc., will yield twelfth grade disciples. The same is true for the ninth and eleventh grade leaders. The last completed grade of the leader will become the highest completion level of the disciple. Sermons, programs, counseling, and even prophecy will all be capped by the minister's lack of educational development. While it may be intriguing and appealing in the beginning, soon the schooled disciple will become frustrated with the obvious deficiencies in the minister and the typical consequences that follow. Thus there is likely to be frequent turnover in the membership and constant wrestles with the leadership for input into the governance of the ministry.

The lightly schooled head is often seriously threatened by the educated disciple and shuns input from him for fear of being exposed and eventually displaced. All these things the well trained apostle knows and takes steps to avert by quickly establishing learning and development as the priority of his ministry and of those who would take on critical roles in it. Hence, the apostolic ministry is more than likely to institute formal educational programs to eliminate the ignorance that has so stigmatized and crippled the Body of Christ over the centuries. Moreover, he will stringently enforce completion and commitment standards upon his learners and followers, and not reward those who disregard it.

2.   Apostles, by now you will agree, are studious, conscientious, scrupulous and exacting. Even if they were called by God unlearned, they burn a good amount of the midnight oil cramming volumes of information in to help them in the dissemination of their truth, and to enhance their credibility to do so. One of the marks of the forthright apostolic personality is self-study. Their early relations with the Lord have made them well aware of His distaste for ignorance. Scripture tells us that God is the God of knowledge, meaning He is the One who dispenses the germs of knowledge the world has propagated. The apostle learns quickly, therefore, that God will tolerate only a limited amount of indifferent, "I don't knows," not followed up by research before He moves on to a vessel with more initiative. This may sound callous, and many Christians may take issue with it, but Jesus told His followers to take heed how they meted out, or used, what they were given. If they did nothing with it, what little they had would be taken from them (Mark 4:24,25). God is the God of increase, and when He finds a minister who will not add to what he learns and is content to coast through his divine service on his limited or stunted education, he allows the servant to run on what he has until he has run out of knowledge and wisdom. If the messenger's purpose is pivotal, then he will seek God for more and it may be granted him.   If not, as we have seen so often, the

messenger will be left to subsist on the remains of what he initially felt was more than enough. The evidence of this is redundant communications and recycled revelations.

Assignment: Apostle RRX needs a ministry tutorial program for five ministers acquired from a ministry merger. What do you recommend, especially since the new comers hate to study and feel their past experience is sufficient?

God's earnest apostles share His attitudes in these areas and are diligent in their efforts to live up to their divine expectations. This makes them trustworthy, reliable, and constant in their pursuit of His knowledge. They do not, as a rule, seek the easy way out; but rather thoroughly embrace God's line upon line, precept upon precept principle of obtaining and increasing knowledge. Moreover, as they acquire it, they do not trifle with treasures of heaven and don't rely on worldly ways of imparting it to others. The power of truth is made known to the apostle emphatically and he harbors no illusions about gray areas, marginal rights and wrongs, or theoretical accuracy. He has come face to face with the eminent power of truth, and the negative, degenerating effects error and lies have on it. The effects weaken its intrinsic strength and jeopardize the messenger's credibility along with the Body's sanctification. The apostle clearly knows both hinder or impede the world's conversion to Jesus. So apostles do not play games with the word of God. Stinging object lessons have taught them the word of truth, first, is God's power and instrument of potency. That is to say, they hate surmising, guesstimates, paraphrasing and the like because they constitute the elements of the lie. The apostle knows their affect is to contaminate the word and thus frustrate its life-giving power by restraining the flows of the Holy Spirit. Paul in 2 Corinthians 2 pointed up his refusal to utilize man's wisdom for Christ's message.

3.   Apostles are, because of the statements made in three above, highly discerning and discriminating. At times their nit-picking can be exasperating and infuriating, but much of it is the product of the rigorous demands placed upon them by the Lord, and oddly enough, the devil who is always lurking for the opportunity to invalidate their efforts. Apostles' powers of deductive reasoning, evaluation, and so on are impeccable once polished, making them persuasive communicators. These abilities become the weapons of their warfare, as well as the tools of their mantle. In addition, being strongly convinced by God of the importance of what they do and its place in His plans, the apostle makes a wary minister. He is cautious about what he accepts, and is critical of what is offered to him. Firsthand disclosures from Jesus on a routine basis make him hard to sway off his place of conviction and harder to dupe with counterfeits of the true. The internal link between them (Christ and His apostles) is so forged that even when the apostle would sway, the iron clad grip of the Lord upon his being renders him unable to turn without the most devastating struggle he has ever had in his life. Even with his strong humbling constraints, the apostle is a remarkably courageous individual. He is resolute and focused. "Be single minded" is his cry for the people of God and for those who serve the people of God. As a result of the fortification of his character, he can be an almost indomitable object in his stead in the kingdom as he goes about completing his assignment.

Suggestion: Give a case example to illustrate the above.

4.   If you read the earlier explanations of the office and the mission of those who fill it, you can well understand why apostles are stern, unwavering, unshakable in their faith or belief. The nature of their induction into Christ's service, coupled with the

mandate they have received from him, weighs heavily upon them. Furthermore, the conditions that necessitate the office leave little room for vacillating ministers. For them the matter is clear, the course is set, the requirement specific, and the prize greatly worth it. The apostle must have impact. He must affect the changes he was sent to ignite. He must bring the people back to the Lord and see they are not rendered disqualified for the inheritance he was sent to preserve them for (Romans 15:16). Apostolic sternness, on top of this, has to do with inside knowledge of the severity of the Lord, a reality Paul had no problem disclosing. While he was well versed in the goodness of God, he held no delusions about the severity of the Lord. The apostle's many visitations with the Lord evidently showed him the God of Israel had not changed. He had not mellowed with age, as modern teachers would have us believe. He merely provided Himself with the one sacrifice that would effectively turn away His wrath against sin, and curtail the consequences of the curse. Nevertheless, woe (as Christ stressed throughout the gospels) to those who trample under foot that last sacrifice. Judging by today's doctrines, it is easy to see why many would like to believe the Apostolic Mantle is done away with. This way they can rest in the libertine "God is love and grace, and liberty for all" message regardless of how a soul treats God. The last thing they want is interference from the Holy Spirit's conviction or fear of retribution. Mental lethargy that lulls the indulgent into practicing the deceptions of sin is their goal. All these the apostle aggressively overturns.

5.   Apostles are extremely self controlled, restrained, and disciplined. They know the power of seduction over the flesh and give no place to it. Paul's remedy? Make no provision for the flesh to fulfill its lust. He and every devoted apostle knows his most dangerous, insidious enemy is the flesh—his own more than any other. So he said he buffeted his body to keep it under the control of the Spirit so that it would not indulge itself in a little helpless, harmless sin now and again. His reasons are seen in Romans 2, as well as in 2 Corinthians. Precious to the apostle is the glory of God and His holiness. Both press the apostle incessantly into conformity, much like Moses in Leviticus 10:10.

6.   The basic nature of this anointing is willfulness, which is destructive apart from the Lord; but when yielded to God, the apostle's old obstinacy becomes an immovable vessel of strength, confidence, performance, and force for His glory. Stubbornness, transformed by the Holy Spirit, then becomes steadfastness in God.

7.   Apostles are compelled by numerous dramatic and somber visions of the Lord. It is due to them that they are awesome combatants in the realm of the spirit. Their resolute nature means they will tackle what must be tackled and get the job done, no matter how strenuous or taxing their assignment is. Apostles have a basic sense of determination that drives them in ways many onlookers, and even those who work for them, cannot understand. Their perseverance and stamina are almost enviable. To this, add the intangibles of shrewdness and insight, and you have the explanation for their high biblical and practical wisdom. Apostles often amaze their contemporaries as they bring joy and deliverance to their followers with their ability to provide the often elusive answers to the perplexities of life. Join this with their staggering perception and you are stunned by the ease with which they unmask the inner secrets of the human heart, exposing the hidden things people cling to, effortlessly. As discomforting as these actions may be, they too are important "qualifiers" of the office. In the hands of the astute and tenderhearted apostle, the exercise of these abilities is with sensitivity, tact, and concern. The absence of proper training has unfortunately caused many to recoil at the Apostolic Mantle, as early officers' inability to

shield the people they minister to with the covering of love has victimized Christ's Body savagely. It has led to the outright rejection of the prophetic in any way. With the restoration of this office, special attention needs to be given to confidentiality, love, tact, and concealment.

Suggestion: Apostle Pros is holding spiritual warfare class, but he has ten students too many. What means of weeding out the unqualified to reduce the class would you recommend?

8.   As with the prophet, for the good of the office, the officer, and those he serves, the apostle too tends to be reclusive. The volume of work the ministry entails and the vastness of their territory mean they often have very few companions. Include in their lifestyle the distance they generate between those they love and what they must minister, and you well understand how for them to be reclusive is self defense. Beyond this, add the constant demand to sit with the Lord to receive the breadth of the enlightenment and the depth of knowledge they need for the mission and you will appreciate the prudence of the apostle's aloofness outside of his service responsibilities.

9.   Apostles are skillful communicators, articulate, and forceful speakers. Again this contributes to the success of leading souls to salvation's repentance, conversion to Jesus Christ, and those once converted to recommit to a holy life of sanctification.

Suggestion: Draft three evangelistic sermons an apostle might preach.

10.   No matter what level, territory, or mandate an apostle is assigned to, he is a strong governor, leader, executive, and business person. It is because they generally start their works where none has been, or with virtually nothing but the skill, wisdom, knowledge, and the power God gives them that the apostle is apt in so many areas. From these they are able to create out of nothing the great things they leave behind in the earth. Those whose mandate is restorative, are no different. They too find that their new move often meets with resistance as it goes against the tide of the status quo. Therefore, they must often make do with much less than their contemporaries and work with fewer and less trained helpers to establish the new thing the Lord wants to do to return those things He has need of back into His control.

11.   Apostles have strong survival instincts, balanced only by an even stronger sense of protection for what is Christ's. His possessions, people, power, and authority all maintain an eminent place in the apostle's heart and mind. His adoration of the Lord makes him unavoidably impatient with reckless Christianity and dangerous doctrinal infiltration. Under these conditions, the stinging rebuke of the apostle is memorable as his whip like tongue and fiery indignation etch a painful reminder in the memory of those who would dare trivialize that which God holds most dear. Oddly, Scripture shows the Lord upheld such fierce defenses as their motivation was love and duty, not—as many ministers strive for—power and control.

A feature of the apostles' mindset that is extremely disturbing to the pseudo and "cosmoschristian" is their unwavering support for the sovereignty of God. It would seem with the wealth of revelations and insight given them, that they would enjoy dissecting, excusing, or belittling the sovereignty of the Lord for their own gain. Actually, the opposite is true. On account of those sweeping disclosures they are often privy to when taken into the confidences of the Lord's, the humble apostle does not seek God's stead; he rather seeks His glory. The apostle does not explain away a perceived evil God has been charged with. He doesn't cover

God's sovereign acts with lame excuses and elaborate tales contrived to spare God the shame of bad publicity. He knows full well that God is not intimidated or affected by the bad press of man. Instead, the apostle takes great pains to teach people who God is and the truth about who and what they are in comparison. He endeavors to console the Lord's beloved with the promises of Scripture without diminishing the Lord's holiness, righteousness, or truth in the process. The apostle who has truly been with Jesus understands the pain of suffering, including God when He must act for His name and righteousness sake. The apostle knows for sure "all things work together for the good to them who love God and are called according to His purpose." In light of this, the apostle survives where many softer ministers fail, and they cause the true church to triumph where the world church corrupts.

12.   If you understood the preceding statements, then this explanation should make great sense to you. Apostles are supernaturally minded, and because of this, uniquely detached from this present world. They understand clearly, its origins, roots, entanglements, and seductions and know what God, Christ, and heaven have to offer in comparison to them. For them there is an enormous disparity between the two. The apostle chooses God over man, the eternal over the temporal, and heaven over earth. As they are heaven minded, they must of necessity be eternally minded. Paul proved this in his message to the Colossians (chapter 3) and Peter did likewise when he spoke about the end of this age, its judgments, and the coming of a new world in which righteousness dwells. (2 Peter chapter 3). No amount of temptation can veer the sincere apostle off his heaven-bound course. His message is replete with visions of heaven, with its raptures and awaiting glories. The worth of its treasures over the corruptibles of this age are vivid to Christ's apostles. One could hardly be a devoted apostle of the Lord Jesus Christ and cling to this world and this age. The reality of Christ's longing for His kingdom and His reign, and the stench of sinfulness and death emitted by this world are an ever crisp vision in the mind of the apostle. Truly his heart is set on pilgrimage.

Suggestion: Design a Bible based teaching on the church's eternal future to present to the class.

13.   Apostles have extraordinary vision. Their pioneering calls mean they have to be great visionaries, as would any founder or restorer. The vision for the mission, the mandate, and above all that, the Lord Jesus' ministry to the world and to His Father all unite in the apostle's soul. They give him the burning ambition he has to see His Savior's work done, and to join Him for the last time having finished that which was committed to his trust. Trust, it should be stressed, is critical to the apostle. He prizes the Lord's trust of him and seeks those of like minds and kindred spirits who will value the trust he must place in them for the good of the mission and the glory of the Lord. All these add to the inspiration the apostle derives from his vision and for it. They communicate to him, they console him, they urge him, and yes, when despair and disappointment set in, they encourage him by reminding him of what his eternal reward and place with the King is in the end.

Suggestion: From what you have learned so far, give three examples of an apostle type vision and how to achieve them.

14.   This should go without saying; however, it is worth reiterating. The apostle's mantle being restored promises the emergence of false apostles. They troubled the early church and as long as the devil remains and man is tied to his sin, they will trouble the

latter churches as well. Therefore, the lines between the true and false need to be sharply delineated. One hard to miss trait of the false apostle is the smooth way they have of indoctrinating the follower to the indulgences of the flesh. Their skill at doing so causes their messages to be received almost without the follower realizing it. They soothingly comfort the restless and dissatisfied flesh of man to assure they never aspire to the holiness that would expose them for what they are: agents of the antichrist. Feeding on the normal discontentment in the soul man, these impostors prepare a feast of carnal indulgence hammering home the world's easy, convenient Christianity and modernized worship. They keep the church's independence and individuality at the fore of their promises and exhortations. Any of these are strong earmarks of false messengers.

Self-salvation, hybrid grace, good works, purchased repentance, a disinterested God, and a multi-lane highway to salvation all testify to their hatred of both the lost soul and the Christ who died to save him. Furthermore, the most damnable part of their ministry is their subtle yet destructive seduction to sin. In imperceptible ways, they promote the loosening of moral restraint. They understand the loneliness that leads one to commit fornication. They can relate to the struggles that cause the sin of adultery to take place. The false messengers sympathize with the weakness that spawns homosexuality, and believe for the carte blanc salvation of the human race. They introduce youngsters to sex early and may be recognized by their stand against guilt (a necessary repentance mechanism) and their redefinition of sin.

It is against the landscape of all these tasty carnal delights that the apostle of Jesus Christ comes to trumpet the call of holiness, purity, chastity, sanctification, sacrifice and commitment. They are known for their strong, rigid, moral, ethical, and righteous standards. Being virtuous, they are avid subscribers to God's standards of veracity, integrity, honesty and rectitude. Jesus' apostles have uncanny judicial instincts that cause them to render peculiarly accurate decisions about those under and around them. Circumstances and events others would find impossible to penetrate, the apostles mental acumen exposes. Their orientations see to it that they have no problem identifying sin and calling it sin. Moreover, their rank in the kingdom gives them the latitude to judge it as Christ has and to condemn its acts and command its censure. Paul made this fact very clear in his writings to explain his ministry and its scope of powers. Apostles, however, do not judge God nor challenge His edicts, decisions, or actions; nor do they apologize for Him either, as if He were some demented or senile parent to make excuses for. Humility and meekness before God is the apostle's way.

Suggestion: Develop a five point teaching on the best strategy for recognizing false apostles and for overturning their effects.

Chapter Five Review 4

1. The personality discussion relates to what?

2. How does personality differ from attributes?

3. What is the relationship of #1 and #2 to the Five-fold Offices?

4. Give the reasons for the apostle's stand on knowledge.

5. Why would the true apostle commit to study and self-education? How is this valuable to Christ?

6. Why is trustworthiness crucial to the apostles mantle?

7. Describe the importance of apostolic discernment.

8. Why is it necessary for apostles to remain stern?

9.   How is restraint and discipline essential to the apostle?

10.   Explain the stubbornness to steadfastness principle that overtakes the apostle's personality.

11.   Discuss the apostle's supernatural interplays with the Lord Jesus.

12.   What is the advantage of the apostle remaining reclusive?

13.   Detail some prominent apostolic abilities and ministry features.

14.   Apostolic sense of duty, defense of Christ, and protection of kingdom treasures is witnessed in and understood to be based on what?

15.   Explain why and how apostles are substantially supernaturally minded.

16.   State the purposes for the apostle's high visionary emphases.

17.   Give a summary of the features of the false apostle's ministry.

The Apostle's Charge and Work

The apostolic call is never to any one church, organization or religious denomination. It is always intrinsically driven to gather out of the secular humanist, and cosmopolitan mainstream those Christ has called. Here is why their mission is to found, restore, establish, and maintain a work and not a church alone. These people are kingdom minded, dominion driven and eternity focused. Matthew 12:30 and Mark 8:34-38 are an excellent testimony of them. For they gather for the Lord and not scatter, and they willingly deny themselves, shoulder their load, and proclaim unflinchingly their Lord and Savior. The Apostolic Mantle cannot be denied or ignored, though many try. One may hate the apostle or love him. He may support him or oppose him. He may resent him or endorse him. But one cannot ignore or miss the Apostolic Mantle in action.

Apostles, moreover, are builders. Therefore, they are compelled to acquire, to build, to expand, and reach for God. They are, because of these inner forces, territorial. They know Satan is ever seeking to displace God's kingdom with sin. Apostles are also dominion minded as they are well educated on the laws, boundaries, and realms God has in place and on how the devil feverishly works to control, infiltrate, and dominate every one. They know his highest aspiration is to overthrow the light with the darkness—to takeover or take back God's possessions; to capture control and seize the reins of power.

The apostle is as jealous for the spheres of God as he is for the glorious manifestations and confirmations of God. He is therefore interested in succeeding in his mandate to regain the land and its souls for the Lord, to give the land rest, to restore righteousness, and to bring the peace of the Prince of Peace to reign in the earth.

One final important thing about the apostle and his call is the discrete elements of his ministry's foundations. The apostle is not an apostle because he starts a work, ignites a move, or founds a church, as with the use of the word *mission* to describe him; these on their own **do not** make an apostle. At best, they reveal and establish him and serve as a means to certify him. However, what makes an apostle is his commission from the king. He is, by definition, "a specially commissioned messenger sent from the face of the king." The apostle's weight and authority all come about through his literal encounter with the Lord Jesus Christ as the risen Savior and glorified Son of Man, Son of God. His means of induction is the basis of his service. The apostle, to be an apostle, must have experienced (and normally experience) Christ face to face to imitate and facilitate his commission. His direct involvement with the Godhead constitutes the essence of his ministry. From these he obtains his message (a mandatory element), derives his revelation, and achieves his teaching. The commission delivers his missions. The encounter releases his message. Repeated intimate encounters shape and define his ministry, and covenant frames his authority before he even undertakes his work.

The Apostle's Work is a Mandate

You have read the word *mandate* used repeatedly throughout our discussions. You probably wonder what it has to do with the apostle. We have already established that the apostle is more than a missionary. We have even gone so far as to show him to be the highest ranking official in the Lord's church and why. We defined what a mission is and gave you its typical elements. Now to tell you about the apostle's mandate. Do you remember when we said the apostolate was a commission? At the same time we also told you what a commission was: that it was a delegate to carry out some specific mission an behalf of another, usually in another country. Well contained in the commission papers we elaborated on is the mandate. That is, the orders and directives that charge the apostle with his duties. They define the parameters of his command, dictate his authorities and powers, and give him instruction an what is to be done on the mission grounds he has been sent to.

Matthew 10 gives you the broadest picture of the Apostolic Mandate, as do several other passages of Scripture. Before he is released by the Lord for the work he has been called to, the apostle is told expressly what his assignment is, how to complete it, who to involve in it, and how to even build it to continue after his demise. The apostle is warned about misuse of his power, abuse of authority, and the consequences of betraying the Lord. As he is vested with his mantle, he is enlightened on the purpose and function of his ministry and Christ's needs concerning it. He is, furthermore, given the promises associated with his obedient success and forewarned that his is not a casual assignment and there are grave prices to pay for dereliction of duty, selfish ambition, and covetousness.

Over the years it took to train the apostle, the Lord has given him samples of His restraining force, and a taste of His chastening. The apostle is not sent out ignorantly; he knows he is specially chosen. As he embarks on his assignment, he knows what awaits him and that the real glory comes much later. With his mantle upon his back, his staff in his hand, and his reward promise in his heart, the apostle bravely sets out on the course that will change the rest of his life and alter him as a person forever.

Apostolic Training

Considering the expanse of the office and its spectrum of powers and authority, the idea of training an apostle must appear ludicrous at this point. How can one effectively train such an officer? The task of defining him is hard enough. Pinning down who and what he is has stymied religious thinkers for centuries. Restraining the forces for the office and its high impact officers is consuming. To release this mantle is risky to every established institution. To suppress it, on the other hand, has proved futile. So what is to be done with him?

With questions like these, largely unanswered, the job of training so formidable a minister is overpowering to the typical educator, and more than a typical educator is required for this work. Yet God, through Christ, managed to get it done and taught the early apostles to do the same. Somehow, the Lord defined the officer, established his rank, and determined his use and role in the Father's plan. He also committed that knowledge to others.

Based upon what the Savior delivered, Peter understood (along with James and John) how to equip their successors to carry on the work the Lord gave them to do. So thorough was this teaching that the newcomer to the order, Saul, was initially schooled by the apostles in preparation for his exhaustive education to come by the Son of God. Together, these two means gave us the wisdom of Paul—formerly Saul—in large portions of the New Testament, which he wrote. Extensive study of the work provides us with great insight into what the Lord taught Paul and what Paul passed on.

His writings lay the foundation and the purpose of the apostle. He, in defense of his ministry, outlines the scope and parameters intrinsic to the office. What the apostle can demand, enact, and institute is shown to us. How he is to be treated, responded to, and supported are all written out in the epistles. The apostolic mindset, his heart and soul, and his ministry concentrations are included to show the distinctives that separate his ministry from the others. God's treatment and expectations of him are recorded to depict the level of interaction he enjoys with the Godhead and the relationship he has with the other officers. How the apostle is charged, chastened, or challenged Paul lets us know, and how the true differ from the false is illustrated. All this information is to be gathered from the succinct writings Paul left us to sort through and classify for the branches of subjects the New Testament must address. Other writers, too, made reference to the apostle. Their contribution sheds further light on the office. Then there is the Lord Jesus Christ who founded and authorized the office. His teachings, subject matter, and themes of importance tell us much about the apostolic view, impact, operations and the like. Combining all these sources together, an orderly method of soundly dispensing the knowledge to others in preparation for their entrance into God's service can be devised. Subjects may be developed and administered the way people generally learn. That is, primary, elementary, intermediate, and advanced level material may be organized and taught at selected intervals. Using customary principles of education, seasoned educated apostles (as the apostolic experience is essential to relevant knowledge impartation) can be trained to rear up others in the ministry.

Again, drawing on the unfolding material the New Testament gives us, a credible means by which the Apostolic Educator can screen students, qualify enrollments, verify knowledge, and confirm readiness may also be developed to maximize both teaching and learning efforts. The program developed may also be enlarged to include critically needed standards and measurements to validate both the education and those educated by it.

Apostolic training is to be stringent, weighty and rigid. The office's high call and heavy responsibility make its training a serious endeavor as its coverage must span the whole of Scripture, integrate proven principles of revelation discovery, and involve extensive activity and experience. Teachers, for these reasons, can only be apostles as they alone can grasp the mainly intangible, yet substantial, elements of the call.

It takes an apostle to explain the seemingly harsh methods God uses to skill and drill the officer. Only the apostle can identify the nuances that make him different, sharper, and still more vulnerable than his counterparts. An apostle with intimate relationship with the Lord can convey the Lord's steely way of introducing him to His unwavering standards of performance, obedience, and exactness. The illuminated apostle can tell of the control signals that warn, chasten, correct, discipline, and restrain the officer of the iron holds of the Spirit he has learned to live with over the years. He can convey the exhilaration of being trusted by God and the degradation of betraying Him.

Along with these vital fundamentals, the apostle can explain the long rope, short chain union the officer has with God: how he is obligated to restrictions, requirements, and regimens the Lord does not and will not ask of the wider part of His Body; and the apostle knows why. To teach it all to a compeer is easier than trying to explain it to others. The internal mechanisms installed by God that make the learner an avid student are absent in the rest of the Body and can make them ridiculing critics. These differences, too, the apostle knows and understands.

Another of the many factors that make the apostle unusual is how he thoroughly apprehends, reveres, and seeks to disclose to others the true mind of God—not as an intelligence principle, a cold judge, a crude disciplinarian; but as a thoughtful, wise, and tender Creator who has been deprived too long of what rightfully belongs to and is due Him. Knowledge like this must be included in apostolic training. He must be well versed in the substance and content of his call and the various particulars it involves. He must know how his message came to be vital, and how he was prepared to deliver it.

The apostle, based on this, is baptized into the message he must introduce and spread. He is intricately brought into the thoughts of God on his work. Naturally, he is not alone in his mission. There are other apostles the Lord has raised up with like minds, insights, and passions to assist him in covering the globe with his movement. These need teaching that prepares them for success with God and man in the ministry. Bringing forth established truth as one rears up the new ministers takes competence. Attracting and enlisting those who share the mandate takes wisdom and appeal. It calls for profound understanding of God and His feelings, ideals, plans, and needs and includes the ability to communicate that understanding responsibly to others convincingly. Such depth of understanding must be accompanied by a rich experience with the Lord to add the wealth of life-giving, hope-inspiring discussion to the classes that keep the training from being dry, academic jaunts and instead makes them fertile learning escapades.

Suggestion: Conceptualize a list of ideal subjects the apostle, at minimum, should have in his or her education. Detail your proposal and state your reasons for your choices.

Chapter Five Review 5

1.   What is the apostle called to?

2.   How do Matthew 12:30 and Mark 8:34-38 enlarge our study?

3.   Explain the mixed responses the apostle may engender and why.

4.   The apostolic nature is what?

5.   The apostle's zeal centers on what?

6.   What is a mandate and how does it relate to the apostle?

7.   How does the apostolate translate to a commission, and why?

8.   What does Matthew 10 add to #7 above?

9.   Summarize the content of the Apostle's Mandate.

10.   Summarize the gist of appropriate apostolic training.

CHAPTER SIX
The Prophet

The Prophet

Introduction

Briefly, we will cover the office of the prophet, so as not to ignore him as a minister of the five Ephesians 4:11 offices. We will not give the prophet here the same attention the apostle received because of the availability of the text frequently referred to, written by this author, entitled *Constructing The Contemporary Prophet*. Its treatment of the subject is so extensive that giving the officer the same coverage here would be redundant. Portions of the recommended text are used occasionally, however, to present you with a good idea of the officer in his place among the remaining five.

The majority of the Bible treatment of the subject of the prophet is contained in the Old Testament. The New Testament in comparison gives little technical or explanative information on this officer. An abridged version of the combined testaments' teaching on the officer and his office is needed to fully comprehend both and their richness.

To begin, the Old Testament provides three Hebrew terms for the English word *prophet*. They are *roeh*, which defines the seer; *chozeh*, which explains the seer who stands in the office of the prophet; and *nabi*, the one who speaks for God by the Spirit's unction. The **nabi** is the customary title used to encompass the entire realm of the Prophet Institution. The word **roeh** enlarges our meaning to include the seeing Prophet's visions and his subsequent oracles. **chozeh** adds the nature and depth of his revelations. Nabi captures the scope of his official function as a spokesman for God whose work is that of the messenger of the Lord. Under the nabi title, we have the preacher of truth (the divine Scripture), doctrinal interpreter, and the holder of supernatural credentials of divine service. The nabi includes the performance or outlet for the supernatural, divine authority, signs and credentials, and a recruitment and teaching mandate to staff and perpetuate the office. Study the following scriptures for examples of these terms: 1 Samuel 9:9, 1 Chronicles 29:29, Isaiah 28:7, 1 Samuel 7, and Exodus 18.

The New Testament gives the one word *prophet* for the three Hebrew terms: *prophetes* collects the **roeh-seer**, **chozeh-revelator**, and **nabi-spokesman** in this one word. Its meanings and characterizations are one and the same; however, their term was initially used to identify those who performed prophetic functions in their nation's pagan religious institutions.

In short, the Greek word *prophetes* defines one who speaks events beforehand—an interpreter of the divine oracles. It includes one used by God to reveal the future and interpret revelations. The *prophetes* declares, unveils, predicts, and shows forth God's will. He or she announces judgments; possesses a unique insight into the divine mysteries of God; and warns His people of the consequences of violating God's laws, will, purposes, and plans.

To start, we will make the clear differentiation between the apostle and the prophet. Let us say both officers are important and their place in the ordained church of Christ is critical. The prophet is second in rank of the five—not because of being viewed by God as less in stature or unimportant, but due to the normal sequence of his emergence in the line organization of the church. Although the prophet may be second, you will encounter many more prophets in the Body of Christ at large than you will apostles. The reason is that God always, under this dispensation, speaks to His church. Besides, God wants to keep His voice alive in the world. So there will always be more prophets throughout the Body than apostles.

In contrast to this, it has been taught in modern church circles that God does not need many prophets; that only a handful per generation are appointed. This persuasion we have shown is very true with the apostle; however, with the prophet it cannot be. The prophet's office is essentially a messenger office. Though he is headquartered in the church of Jesus Christ, his ministry overflows into the world. Those who do not know God benefit on account of this, as much from the prophet's mouth as from God's family. The Lord intends for it to be that way. Next we will look at some of the problems with this view and the bases for the fallacies they engender in the minds of the people, the largest one being prophets called of God holding back from God for fear of being out of order. The consequence of this is the chastening of rebellion the Lord delivers to all who defy His commands. The following analysis may help you see things differently. If you are among the many hold outs that have fallen victim to this short sighted view, perhaps after reading it you will stand up and boldly take your place with the emerging army of prophets gathering today.

How Many Prophets Does a Responsible Lord Need?

The prophet's office covers not only the Pentecostal and Charismatic Movements, but it covers and addresses the entire Body of Christ, explaining why there are power prophets and strictly or mainly oracular prophets. Power prophets take it upon themselves to believe that the entire office is committed to their trust alone; that God does not want to communicate or keep relevant truth in front of any other group except themselves. Yet understanding the nature of the Lord, one could see this is not the case. God says He shines His sun on the just and the unjust, on the good and the evil. This being true, the Lord's righteousness compels Him to speak to the nations to warn them, as well as to the church. Historically, the Bible shows us how God has always spoken to the world and His people. He desires that none should perish. For the Pentecostals and the Charismatics to confine the revelation of God's truth to only themselves and believe that they alone are charged with its dispensation is narrow and sadly selfish. God is a great God who loves all His creatures. He desires to make contact with and to answer every one of them. He has decreed that He will answer all who sincerely call on Him. God also said He would make Himself known to the inhabitants of the earth. Consider, on the basis of these revelations, how many prophets God would need today and perhaps for the next several generations.

Statistics suggest that there are approximately six billion people on the planet. Let us say that God would need only 1% of the population to be His voice to the others. That means for the Lord not to be understaffed in this area, He would need no less than sixty million prophets worldwide. Statistics further show that the Pentecostals, as a whole, do not even number sixty million; meaning by this, that if every confessing Pentecostal in the world were a prophet—a bona fide Scripture-defined prophet—there would be a deficit of somewhere near fifteen million or so prophets. Do see how many souls would be deprived of a dire word from the Lord when needed? Ask yourself, can you really see the Alpha and Omega being that much understaffed?

To continue, why not say we deduct from the sixty million the false prophets, and those who have only the gift of prophecy in operation. Wouldn't you say, if that took away two thirds of the sixty million, a need for at least ten million prophets would exist if we adjusted our number to factor in pastors and apostles taking up some of the load? At bare minimum, the number of prophets God needs to have ready and trained would fill a small state or a medium-sized city to keep a qualified voice from God available to answer the needs of persons in all walks of life.

America alone, if she were to be fully covered prophetically, would need at least a half million prophets. Using the same factors we used above, a good 100,000 would be the base minimum. Unless they are all underground, there are nowhere near that amount of recognized prophets organized throughout the country. You can believe there are several times that amount of false prophets brazenly declaring who they are and why they exist. It is interesting how Christ's church's narrow mindedness plays right into the hands of darkness. We can often be charged with sabotaging the Lord's mission ourselves. It is a pity that we cannot meet the Lord's "all walks of life" objective with the prophet, as well as with the pastor, teacher, and evangelist. The key to the last sentence is the phrase "all walks of life." The Lord's voice must be heard in all areas of human life. Every field, every profession, every industry, every community, neighborhood, and household must have an available prophet to see that God's voice is sounded and His truth publicized. The aggressive move to silence and depose the prophet (and the apostle) means the officer's presence has been scaled off from the masses. On account of this, the normal number of messengers for the job must increase to eradicate the damage done by the flood of false messengers who have been the supernatural stronghold in place of God's ministers. To understand this better, read over the Old Testament record of prophet abuse and the institutions of orders of Baal (Satanists). These prophets' campaigns were so successful against the truth that the people believed their words were from the mouth of the Lord. These counterfeits of the true brought untold reigns of terror and harm upon the people of the Lord repeatedly. At fateful intervals in Israel's turbulence, the Lord would raise up, for example, an Elijah who would establish a school of prophets to train others to take up the mantle and fight for the cause of Jehovah.

For several decades the true prophet would rule and stand as not only the watchman, but as a blockade against the efforts of darkness. So long as the people relished truth, they would fear the Lord and right would reign. When they became tired of obedience, the people would desire a loosening of Jehovah's reins in favor of a little sin. It was at these times that the Lord would find the people turning against Him and on His prophets. Lawmakers would rise up and relax the laws that hindered the move toward apostasy or that harmed their popularity. Entertainment would lead the pack with titillating seductive amusements to drench the social consciousness in envy, lust, covetousness, and discontentment. Education would take up its banner by training the culture's heart in the covetousness they craved. Religion would be the last hold out. It would respond for mainly economic reasons, with a softening of its stand on the vital issues of immorality and godlessness. Over time the nation's godly moorings would deteriorate and wide scale suffering would occur as the people's sinfulness brought the reproach of God upon them and their land.

Once the season of sin had run its course and the land was in the grip of atrocious human suffering and despair, the cry would go up for God to intervene. It was through the prophets that the Lord did so. God would send them with His message to repent, receive salvation, turn from their wicked ways, and He would heal their land.

History will show the cycle is the same, remaining unchanged generation after generation. For thousands of years it has happened, and it will go on until the end of this age. Prophets, as you can well understand by now, became even more plentiful during those periods of humanity's dark ages—ages where the lights of righteousness are snuffed out by the passions of sin. When sin's hold on them sways, men begin to seek the Lord and call for His prophets. Then the dawn of a Prophetic Era appears as people suddenly realize they are helpless; that there is a God who cares and can help. It is at this time they begin to turn to Him and wide scale revival breaks out. Prophets begin to swarm the land and flock together for assignments and dispatch. They disperse worldwide, thereafter, to the territories the Lord sends them.

Delighted, the post apostate generation suffering the blows of what their parents caused embrace God's prophetic movement as relief from the brunt of judgment heaped upon them for their sin. Thus, you have the motivation behind the new moves of God and the reasons the prophets play a critical role in them.

Suggestion: Review the previous material and outline the conditions and situations existing today that verify the need for the prophet and that signal God's impending move.

Chapter Six Review 1

1.   Explain the perpetual worldwide need for prophets, and why.

2.   Describe the shifts to Baal Prophets.

3.   Describe what provokes an apostate nation's return to God.

4.   How does #3 translate to revival?

What is a Prophet?

A prophet is first, and beyond all else, **the mouthpiece of God—His spontaneous messenger**. In addition, as an expression of this prime duty, the prophet is a *front line warrior, a watchman, intercessor, and governor* of the church of Jesus Christ. He enters the realm of the spirit and peers behind the veil of the supernatural to a) conduct the warfare needed to protect and defend the flock of God; b) patrol the supernatural to guard and keep the people of God; c) intercede for (that is to stand in the gap on behalf of) those beaten down, enslaved to, or otherwise afflicted as a result of the forces of darkness that seize the liberty of saints from time to time; d) oversee, legislate, and adjudicate the mishaps and missteps of the church of the Lord; e) Translate and apply current events to ancient prophecy.

Prophets are empowered by a number of organs, their prophet spirit being the principal one. All prophets share the same spirit field of God. That means each one of them were given at creation a portion of the prophetic side of God's make up in anticipation of Adam's fail and man's subsequent need to hear from God out of the depths of human alienation and darkness. Different personalities make up the attributes that distinguish them as individuals, but the prophet spirit is detectable by any astute person and by all other prophets. By prophet spirit we mean the supernatural core of emission that emanates from those whose intangible character is destined to interact with the supernatural world on a consistent basis. Scripture tells us, in the book of James, that it is the spirit that gives life to the flesh. Jesus confirms this statement in John's Gospel. Lastly, we are taught by God in His Word that all He does and releases is first spirit-initiated or spirit-originated. For the prophet it is no different.

The presence of his spirit will be detected many times without effort on his part. When Jesus was talking with the woman at the well, the woman said to Him, "I perceive that thou are a prophet." More than once was Jesus recognized as a prophet. How? By the spirit of the prophet that was in Him.

A number of intangible faculties are used to discern a prophet. Perception, alertness, cognizance, astuteness, intuition, and acumen are all faculties used to discern his spirit, the apostle's spirit, and the other officers also, for that matter. Paul talked about the prophet's spirit in the book of 1 Corinthians. He stressed that the prophet was able to control his. Jeremiah referred to the spirit of the prophets as well. Many references were made to this significant possession of the prophet, and it is implied that all servants of God are disposed to their ministries according to the nature and predisposition of their spirit, and the dispensations of the Holy Spirit in accordance with them. Understanding this alone will tell you why a person cannot fulfill equally the required dispensations of more than one office at a time. Other grounds for the spirit's importance are seen in the number of times it is mentioned, and in the necessity for it being present to empower a prophet to stand in the office.

Today, when prophets meet each other, only a few moments of conversation need be exchanged before they can perceive the kindred prophet spirit shared by them both. In cases where the Holy Spirit is doing the arranging, there need be no words spoken at all. One or the other will pick up the spirit of the prophet between them, or the Holy Spirit will supernaturally reveal it.

Succinctly speaking, the prophet is the mouth of the Lord. This definition is first understood from God's preparation of Moses for the office, found in Exodus.

Another basic word for prophet comes from the Greek *pro* and *phanei*, which means "to speak beforehand." The prophet, therefore, speaks (reveals an event, predicts) something before it happens. He unveils what God has shown him will happen. Under the New Testament of Jesus Christ, many people can do this sometimes or in certain conditions because they have the Holy Spirit living within them. It is essential to say that being able to say what will happen in advance from time to time is not the only thing that makes a prophet.

The prophet has, in addition to this fundamental ability, an unusual authority. His authority is mainly spiritual but is felt very strongly in our natural world. This is why people dread him and often avoid his ministry. It is also why the devil has convinced so many people today that the prophet should not exist or should be fought. Because of the mantle of God's authority upon him, people unavoidably listen to the prophet and respect what he says. What makes their authority even more impelling is the consistency in which the words they prophesy come to pass. When a person can accurately predict from God what will happen always, then the Bible says they are a prophet and should be feared; that is, respected and esteemed, and heeded.

As a result of their prophetic authority, prophets hold the strange ability to move people to obey. When people oppose them, God stands up for them to defend their words, their work, their ministry, and their assignment because their words were His. To disobey God's prophets is to disobey God (2 Chronicles 20:20).

God presents Himself to the prophet usually through a dream or a vision. Most prophets have a history of dreams and visions throughout their life. It is not until the Lord manifests their ordained call that they understand them as a divine resource to be used in their professional ministry. Numbers 12 records God stressing this as a sign of a prophet's induction to His service. Following this, dreams and visions become more frequent and their substance more pronounced in the prophet's life. Once the Lord has made Himself known to the prophet, understanding and insight are awakened in him. He now recalls and maintains his dreams more easily. He can often find that he understands their basic meaning. These are all signs of his call to be used by God.

In addition to dreams, the prophet also takes on a new dimension of hearing. He can now hear things from the spirit realm, as God makes His voice audible to him. He can hear instructions from the Holy Spirit, overhear spiritual comments from the devil, and the prophet can hear on many occasions the voice of the human heart. The prophet receives, on top of these, special revelations from the Lord. He can hear in retrospect, the present, and in the future in a moment of time. When he is ministering to a person, the prophet can periodically hear their memory, their hopes, their history, their hurts, and so on by the Holy Spirit's faculties within him. These are known as the prophet's perceptive revelations.

The prophet can either see his revelation or he can hear it. Both are means of prophecy. Seeing the revelation is a higher form, as it requires interpretation to translate the vision into the understanding of another. Translating spiritual messages is another customary ability of the prophet. Their translation faculty includes deciphering symbols, songs, types, shadows, and signs. Prophets are also visionaries. That means they can see spiritual things that others cannot see. When they cannot see them, they can discern them. The prophet's spiritual endowments enable him to pull back the curtain of the natural world, or break through it with his spiritual eye, and pick up the presence of immaterial beings. The Holy Spirit helps the prophet to do this; however, many people who don't have the Holy Spirit because they do not serve the Lord Jesus Christ can still exercise these spiritual gifts. This is because their prophet talents and abilities are part of their natural make up. They are only made better when the Lord sanctifies them and purifies them for His use.

Prophets are very strong and are often stern people who give the world spiritual messages. They also work miracles and get in touch with the supernatural world to handle its affairs for the people around them. Without God this is illegal, but with His prophets it is very necessary. Study Isaiah 8:19-22; Jeremiah 23; Hosea 6:5; and Isaiah 47:13. Intercession is also a gift and a cardinal responsibility of the prophet. This is where one person prays to God or wrestles with spiritual enemies for another. For the prophet, intercession is a large part of his work. People are always in need of his help in tackling the invisible forces that hate man so. Prophets are among the best people for the job.

To be a prophet takes many years, although one may be called to the office early after salvation. To learn God, however, and to understand His ways and the ways of the supernatural takes time. Many people do not want to spend the time, which is unfortunate because the better you are prepared the better you will succeed when it comes time to help someone with (or through) your abilities, or when it comes time to be used of God.

Prophets sometimes work miracles, as we have said, but not all of them. Those who do not have the baptism of the Holy Spirit or who do not value their baptism will not be able to work miracles for God, although they will be able to speak His words from their spirit because they were born with the prophet spirit. Those prophets who cannot work miracles are called **oracular prophets**. That means they only speak from the mouth of God, but display no supernatural power. John the Baptist, Daniel, Jeremiah, Ezekiel, and a number of others were oracular prophets. New Testament prophets have the Holy Spirit in them and may receive miraculous help from Him, but this is not the same as having the Lord implant a supply of miracle seeds in you for service at the appropriate time, and orientating you officially to the stead of a miracle worker as part of your normal prophetic duties.

For more in-depth information on the prophet and his ministry, get the recommended textbook on this subject.

Chapter Six Review 2

1.   The prophet's office covers what? Addresses what?

2.   Name the two types of prophets.

3.   Explain the common misconception concerning prophets and why it is wrong.

4.   How many prophets does God need? Why?

5.   Discuss prophet abuse.

6.   What causes a prophetic rule or reign, and how is it overthrown?

7.   Give seven features of the prophet.

8.   Explain the prophet's spirit.

9. How is the prophet's spirit discerned?

10. Greek and Hebrew names for the prophet are what? What do they mean?

11. What alone does not make a prophet?

12. What unusual ability does the prophet have and how does it affect others?

13. How does God present Himself to the prophet?

14. What new dimensions does the inaugurated prophet take on?

15. Discuss the prophet's revelatory gifts and abilities.

16. How is #15 different in unregenerate prophets?

17. Special messages and miracles have what to do with the prophet? How and why?

A Few Points About The Prophet

l. A prophet is expressly a messenger officer, where the apostle, in comparison, is a builder with a message. Founding may or may not be the call of the prophet, but it is *always* the call of the apostle. Not all prophets move in the miracle signs and wonders of God. As in the Old Testament, some are strictly espousers of God's truth and discerners of God's movements. Although, as with any believer with the Holy Spirit's baptism, there may be manifestations such as those listed in 1 Corinthians 12. They are to be distinguished from the regular and liberal use and/or inherent power that characterize the Apostolic Ministry, and the Power Prophet's Ministry.

2. The prophet can be a visionary, but with very limited scope in contrast to the object and impact of the apostolic vision. Nevertheless, visions are a key function of the prophetic ministry. Their visions center on situations rather than projects, ordinarily. They see incidents, events, history, or mysteries as the mainstay of their ministry, as distinguished from the primary founding, organizing and constructing/implementing focus of the apostle.

3. The Prophet receives communications from God in visions, dreams, by impressions, or through his supernatural capacity to interpret instincts or read situations or events. He may also hear from the realm of the spirit or merely pick up supernatural activity relative to his assignments and service.

4. Itinerant in nature, prophets generally will never be just pew warmers. They are assigned by Christ to several congregations or denominations at once. Their ministry can be said to be Body wide. That is, wherever there is reverence and respect for the Lord and a verification of the authenticity of the prophet, they will be accepted and welcome in a church. Here is what Christ is talking about when He says "receive a prophet in the name of a prophet to receive a prophet's reward." The reason for this promise is obvious. The nature of the prophet's job is unpleasant to the sinner, and therefore, they are shunned more often than not. Throughout scripture, it has been noted that the most abused of the leaders of Israel were the prophets. Today it has not changed much. While in our part of the world they do not throw literal stones or physically shove the prophet out of the doors of the church, the horrendous spiritual and figurative mistreatment he has received over the years, amounts to the same thing. Since the office has yet to continue until this age is finished, the Lord provided an incentive to not only welcome, but to receive the ministry of the prophet as well: "Protect him, support him, respect him, shield him; and what the prophet will receive for his faithfulness, you shall receive also for your faith." This is the substance of the message.

5. The prophet is a probing, discomforting minister. He can be mysterious, though not mystical. When the group is lively, he is subdued. When they are subdued the prophet is excited. When the subject is superficial the prophet retreats to the spirit of his depths. When it is profound, the prophet is piercing. He is ever watching, meditating, listening, and digging into the silent, secret things of God and His creation. He scans the subtle in an instant and registers information easily overlooked by the majority. The prophet is a thinker, ever comparing, analyzing, and relating seemingly insignificant facts and details to widen his scope, to glean more from God, or to prepare for his next assignment. The

110

prophet is a forward moving individual who is ever at the next stop while others are resting at the last one.

6. Like the apostle, the prophet is more God-minded in service and devotion than people-minded. Most prophets, however, make terrible people-persons, making them the most impatient and disinterested pastors you are likely to find. If they have good right hands, you may never know this. But if they are forced to interact with the flock extensively and directly, they are bound to be discovered as not the shepherding type. Prophets are more God-obsessed than people-impressed. The prophet's heightened intelligence, lofty experiences with the Lord, and perpetual inner vision makes him lose patience with the mundanity he feels consumes the average life. Unless he is with comparable peers, he is likely to be the poorest conversationalist. He seems bored with most everything, but really he is more aloof than anything else. His nature is distant as his thoughts helplessly escape to the realms where he is most comfortable: the thoughts and mind of God, at every opportunity.

7. Prophets tend to be detached loners. Much of this has to do with their need to be with and feed from the Lord. Highly sociable prophets are a rarity and one wonders how they can mingle intimately with the people and still be effective in their positions. Scripture shows us that prophets generally could not be found among the masses, but they were off somewhere alone, listening for and to the voice of God. If it is not one of these two, then they were off on a mission for God.

8. Prophets, too, are known for incisive judgment and discernment, as the need for rendering decisions in the name of the Lord about His righteousness and truth (or the lack of it) in human matters is frequent. Their constant spiritual wanderings make them ready to deliver their judgments seemingly in an instant. More often, they have very likely seen the matter in God before it came to their earthly attention, and so they appear rash in their responses at times. This can prove an irritation to others who think them impulsive or show offs, when in fact, the Lord's supernatural preparation has enabled them to be decidedly swift in their analyses and understanding.

9. Undisturbed usually by the odd requirements of the office—and oddity does characterize this office—the prophet learns early to go with the strange demands of the Lord. Especially attuned to symbolism and imagery as a means of receiving communication from God, the prophet is quite good at interpreting the signs or symbols he or she receives as messages from the Lord. Interpretation, by the way, is only justified in these instances. Acting out what the Lord has shown them as prophecy is a normal means of prophetic communication and is used to reinforce visually the audible impacts of what God would say to provoke the faith or obedience of the recipient.

10. Prophets are articulate communicators with great personal, emotional, and psychological restraint when seasoned and well trained. Those who take God and their mantle seriously will not give in to the carnal temptation to blab all they know and see, or to exploit the ministrations of God. Among the many early lessons they receive, timing and patience rank high on the list of practices the Lord would have prophets cultivate. Yielded prophets are stringently taught, and when sincere, eagerly practice waiting on the Lord and sensing His times and seasons. Only immature and untrained prophets fling caution to the wind in favor of self-exaltation and ego. The prophet's norm is to let God lead and the prophet gratefully follow.

11. Prophets tend to be daring, challenging, and dynamic in their service to God and their witness of the Lord Jesus. They have the unnerving way of stretching out on the Lord and dragging those around them on the limb with them. Many times, this is not the initiative of the prophet as much as it is the propulsion of the Lord. Because of the Lord's extraordinary grip on the spirit and soul of the prophet, He can move him to the middle of high tide or the brink of apparent disaster without the prophet being aware of it until he is in the thick of it all. The Lord's ability to sop the prophet in His omnipotent strength and faith has him doing the magnificent, the spectacular, and seemingly reckless without the prophet's cognizance. The prophet's adventures with God are typically so exhilarating, however, that he enjoys the staggering awesomeness of God and His use of him in ministry.

12. The Prophetic Mantle is confrontational, as we can see from the examples given us in Scripture. The messenger is ever having to confront the agents of Satan, antichrist behaviors and trends, and similar subtle attacks on the sheep of the Great Shepherd. They must engage in heretical conflicts and wrestle with endless controversy over doctrine, dogma, tradition, and the commandments and controls of men over the people of God. Prophets find they are repeatedly in the deliverance mode as the flock of God regularly succumb to the flesh, stray to the world, explore sin, and strain against the righteousness of God. Christian duty and commitment to the church and its growth in the kingdom's virtues and graces often falter and flail and must be spiritually and potently fortified to stabilize them on many occasions.

13. The prophet's office is a preaching-teaching ministry, whereas the apostle's office is generally the opposite, a high teaching ministry that preaches. The prophet emphasizes preaching over teaching since inspired utterance dominates the flow of his messages. Prophets, nevertheless, can be able teachers, if you encounter those who enjoy research and study equally as much as they enjoy drinking from the wells of the Holy Spirit of God. Some prophets take too much delight in exclusively hearing from the realm of the spirit rather than seeking and learning God from His Word. These prophets tend to be weak in truth, limited in prophetic scope, and more emotionally unstable than the others. Moreover, they are restricted in the range and depth of prophecy they can deliver and narrow the field of prophetic matters they can effectively officiate to a skimpy minimum.

14. Prophets who really understand their office and its gravity are scrupulously obedient. They too possess a frank awareness of the severity of the Lord and His consequences for disobedience in service. The Lord does not take lightly the unfaithfulness of His servants, especially in those placed in critical offices where their actions affect many with rippling effects that can span years.

15. The prophet's anointing has a staunch chastening and correctional component attached to it that many resent. Their persuasive, power packed preaching is convicting in and of itself. Add to this the influence of. their authority, their dynamic presence, and the exemplary delivery that pervade the office's executions and you have a no-nonsense minister with no qualms about following up God's words with discipline. This anointing is what marks their ability to motivate repentance and provoke obedience where so many others fail. Ideally, the prophet will be a strong proponent of manifesting the fruit of the Spirit in conjunction with the whole counsel of God. When added to all else you would see the marvelous mix of righteousness, holiness, love, truth, and compassion the church feels

cannot be accomplished by those who take the entire Bible as the word of God. Balance, wisdom, restoration, and soundness would characterize such a ministry and its minister.

16.   Prophets, too, are relatively judicial in the nature of their service. Prophetic judgment cannot he overstated and should not be underestimated. Those well trained handle the nuances of God's Word expertly, and when linked to their superior spiritual insight and practical depth, they are more than accurate in their assessment of matters pertaining to the kingdom of God and its life and holiness. Prophets cannot help but call sin what it is and judge that which God has defined in His Word. Not to do so would make them derelict in the discharge of their duties and incompetent in the affairs of their office.

Chapter Six Review 3

1. Explain the builder with a message analyses.

2. Comment on visionary prophets.

3. What is the problem with the prophet as a pew warmer?

4. What makes the prophet a discomforting minister?

5. Describe prophets' devotion.

6. Why are prophets generally loners?

7. Detail the office's oddities and their significance.

8. Discuss the nature of prophets' verbal skills.

9.   How is the mantle confrontational?

10.   Preaching emphasizes the prophet's ministry. Tell how and why.

11.   Obedience is important to the officer—how and why?

12.   Chastening and correction feature prominently in the prophetic anointing for what reasons?

13.   Address prophets' judicial nature and its importance.

The Prophet's Personality

1.   Prophets can be quite stand-offish, and as pointed out earlier, strangely distant. As associates they are usually not inclined toward the high sociability that most people enjoy. Small gatherings, informal fellowship get-togethers, and long intimate interactions with trusted friends appeal to them more than high visibility entertainment. A number of things can account for this, but the main one is the prophet's special union with God. He sees amusements in a way others do not. God's stand on idolatry, for instance, is particularly pressing on him. The prophet cannot view things as harmless and simple entertainment as most people can. He is forced to, by his yoke, look at the roots, origins, and influences surrounding the amusement. Statues, puppets, cartoons characters, and activities all take on deeper meanings for the God- attuned prophet. Even the holidays he has grown up to embrace and revere are challenged by the prophet as he weans himself from the things of this world. Humor, celebrations, and diversions of the world all undergo intense scrutiny by the spiritually enlightened prophet. This tends to offend people and makes it difficult for them to relate to the prophet or to plan any affairs around him. If this trait of theirs is not handled with tact, it can increase the alienation the prophet experiences as people's aversion to his rigidity will lead them to shun him. Tactless responses to the things unenlightened people hold dear can shut critical doors prophets need to set captives free from the seductive delusions of Satan. Doing so is only beneficial when the motivation is from God and not the prophet's own motivation.

Suggestion: Give a sketch of the situations that are related to the above.

2.   The office calls for a strong, forceful personality with a solid identity in the Lord Jesus. The prophet devoid of his Christ identity is a prophet who will squander his endowments and anointings. The mind of Christ is crucial to the church as a whole. For the prophet, the fullness of Christ is a must for success. Allegiance, faith, obedience, surrender, and reliability all hinge upon the prophet's right identification with himself in relation to the Savior If the prophet has not resolved this before he has entered full time ministry, he will likely fumble in his early years and stumble into sin. If he thinks himself an independent entity in association with the Lord Jesus Christ and His mission and aims, the prophet will fall prey to the Balaam concept of his ministry. He will easily sell himself and his Lord out to the highest bidder. The prophet who does not understand the nature of the ministry in general, the prophetic ministry in particular, and the mentality of the Lord Jesus in regard to it, will not serve Christ faithfully or for long. Such a prophet; as a result of these shortfalls, will not be forceful, determined, persevering, or steadfast. He will exhibit a timid, vacillating, indecisive, or disinterested attitude in the mantle he wears and in the reason God instituted it in the first place.   Moving by the Spirit, or any spirit, will be his chief drive.

   The prophet will, furthermore, reflect unfeeling arrogance about why the Lord called him to be a prophet, dishonoring the office altogether. High carnality, humanism, bias, traditionalism, and legalism are likely to abound in his ministry. Meanwhile, the immaturity of those he serves will not be significantly affected by his labors.

Suggestion: Draft a profile of actions and attitudes that illustrate this point in service.

3.   Though meek before God, the office exhibits a confident, rough exterior that conceals the soft, tender underbelly. Impressive boldness is a feature of the prophet's presence. The prophet often has to hide his tender side to execute the will of the Lord concerning the lives of those he serves. He is, of necessity, usually a gentle soul and would enjoy life and people as much as anyone else. If left to himself, the typical prophet would recoil at

the idea of ruffling the waters of life. The ministry he bears, however, will not permit him to do so. He must maintain a certain detachment to remain objective and impartial in his renderings. The forced detachment he must keep often expresses itself in an abrasive, stiff way. Many, many times, this simply is not the truth. The prophet does care but has learned that he must prioritize his affections. The higher devotions, he knows, must always go to the Lord if he is to continue to live out the tough choices he constantly is obliged to keep in faithfulness to his call. Self-centered observers impulsively take this as prophet arrogance or superiority and rebel against much of the prophet's efforts. Consequently, they retaliate with vengeful behavior spawned by the resentment they feel at imagined slights and abuses they project onto the prophet.

4. The personality of this minister appears to be defiant and even radical. In many ways the prophet is this way; however, it is because the demands of the office call for a fiery military stance on the issues it must face and oppose. The prophet of the Lord Jesus Christ strongly resists sin, and therefore has a disturbingly low tolerance for its manifestation. Their standard of righteousness spontaneously moves them to revolt against it almost as a reflex action. Their sharp tongue snaps rebukes, correction, and censure unflinchingly—even before the officer has had time to restrain his reaction. His offensiveness at the sin laxity on the part of the Body of Christ is motivated by the inevitable displeasure of the Lord.

5. The prophet's physical being is rugged and they are doggedly faithful to the purpose and function of their call. They typically finish what they start and complete the mission they embark on. Doing so regularly puts them face to face with the fiercest hardship, which experience has taught them is normal in the Lord's ministry.

Suggestion: Research and identify three prophetic examples of #5, and relate their situations and how you found them relevant.

6. The demands for the office call for the prophet to be somewhat mysterious with a strong leaning toward the supernatural habitually. One noteworthy thing about the prophetic anointing is that it works all the time; this is so much so that the Lord often has to call his attention to the importance of a particular communication from time to time to distinguish it from the constant stream of information the prophet is accustomed to receiving. By the same token, the idea some people have that the prophet can predict, prophesy, or minister otherwise at will is wrong. Spontaneous utterances are definitely as the Spirit wills. Although the prophet is able to divulge some tidbit he may have picked up from the Lord during earlier conversations or past revelations, blurting them could be hazardous and reckless. These the prophet is wise to submit to the will of the Lord instead of the leading of his own spirit. Without question, he can speak what he perceives, discerns, and discovers in the person's spirit. Still, what he utters may not be prophecy but perception. The prudent messenger would be more responsible if he cultivated the practice of moving by the Holy Spirit if these disclosures are not the product of being caught up in the ministerial anointing.

7. Like apostles, and as most ministers should have, prophets have high moral, ethical, and righteous standards. For them to be the first partaker of the word of the Lord, if they are sincere, it is a must. As a result, the prophet can be intolerant and unyielding on matters pertaining to the believer's sin. They especially dislike the flagrant abuse of Christian liberty toured as a covenant right today. Prophets can make those around them

quite uncomfortable if they are in the habit of living in the gray areas of life and of insisting on double standards for themselves and others. Prophets are firm about the truth of God, the black and white of His Word, and the obligation of every vessel of His Spirit attaining to its expression in lifestyle and their attitude. Free morality, libertine fidelity, and indulgence in the flesh all disturb the devoted prophet for whom the lines God has drawn between Himself and the works of darkness, which are vividly clear.

8.   The gravity of the office and the somberness of the message prophets often have to deliver make them very serious people with earthy wisdom. Also, their knowledge of God's character and holiness, coupled with their understanding of the folly of personal sin, makes them intolerant or the frivolity of the flesh. Playfulness, worldliness, and secularism are generally not traits you will find in God's prophet, although he can have a great sense of humor. A frankness and straightforward delivery of the truth makes his messages at times quite humorous, useful to take the sting out of some of the more severe themes.

Suggestion: Sketch three biblical and two modern instances of earthly prophetic wisdom.

9. Prophetic sincerity causes these ministers to despise compromise, spiritual apathy, and carnal indulgences. They fight the foolish flirting with seductions that make the saint vulnerable to satanic forces and to the judgment of God. Genuine prophets detest fence straddling and the middle-of-the-road Christianity modern converts delight in. The prophet further calls for a strong commitment to either sin or God, but like Christ in the Book of Revelations, spurns most the lukewarm Christian.

10.   Prophets are normally apt to teach. There are teaching prophets whose ministry concentrates on rearing up other prophets, and there are prophets with the natural gift of teaching whose sermons are substantially informative rather than inspirational. For these reasons, the diligent prophet is studious. He even disciplines himself to try his revelations and to prove the words he receives from the realm of the spirit to assure they are from the Lord and remain biblically founded. Prophets with integrity are self-restraining and unusually patient enough to be careful not to run ahead of God in prophecy revelation. This, no doubt, is an outcome of always having to wait on the Lord for the discrete nuggets of truth that take their time coming forth into this natural realm, as well as their natural understanding.   Such conditioning no genuine prophet can achieve without or avoid.

11.   Similar to the apostle, the prophet too is a skillful and strategic warrior. He is formidable in warfare, as his most momentous periods in ministry can happen in spiritual combat. Prophets, as we have said earlier, are intercessors who reach into the supernatural kingdoms to retrieve that which belongs to the people of God in the natural. To be triumphant at these times, the prophet has to clash with the demonic guardians holding onto the blessings. Spiritual education and practical drills by the Holy Spirit have made him proficient in confrontation and competent in the miraculous maneuvers called for to overturn the strongholds of darkness and to cut a path in the heavenlies so the outpourings of God flow.

12.   Prophets are peculiarly yielded to the will, moods (and mood swings), and temperaments of God. The meshing of the prophetic faculties of God with the capacities of the prophet lifts them to the lofty heights of worship and communion that makes for the intimacy and trust that releases power in action. Constant admiration of the divine glories keeps them remote from the superficial longings of natural man. When it comes

to worship in the earthly sanctuary, this is really true. Here is why you often find the prophet strangely detached from a particular worship and praise service they happen to be sitting in. God's present mind toward the meeting is uppermost in the sensitivity of the prophet. It does not matter that the people are receiving a different dispensation. The prophet is ever geared by God for His next move. So joy may be the mood of the meeting, while the prophet is switched on to God's impending outpouring which may be heaviness, warning, or some other emotion or manifestation. He is unable to settle in, all the time, the present expressions the masses may be enjoying because of his unvarying interlink with the motions of God.

Suggestion: Write from biblical and historical research the gist of what this section is talking about and follow with a four-point guide to recognize this expression in effect.

13. Poetry, music, psalms, and odes are likely to characterize many prophets' ministries. These activities vent the ministry of this office, as it tends to flow and intensify under highly aesthetic conditions. The proper blend of praise and worship effectively release certain distributions of the Holy Spirit that would be otherwise hindered by dry, barren atmospheres.

Suggestion: Identify one or more biblical examples of the effect of the prophet's music ministry.

14. Prophets must be objective and impartial. Genuinely groomed prophets cannot tolerate favoritism, a quality that strongly influences their break with family ties and imposing relationships. Their reasons have little to do with personal integrity or natural liberality, but more so with the Lord's revelations and insistence upon unity in His Body. These are seen by God as an attestation of the true new creation spirit of His families. To stretch out with any depth in the kingdom of God and to be trusted with His awesome dominions, the prophet is challenged to put away his carnal and cosmos perspectives and glorify God by accepting the work of His Son in its absolute totality.

Suggestion: Draft a case where a prophet must confront and overturn bias. Include how he discerns it and the means by which he identifies it in action.

15. Prophets are rigid, concise, crisp thinkers with strong powers of discrimination and reason. As we have seen above, because of this they must guard against narrow mindedness and bigotry. Prophets can easily become inflexible, obstinate personalities which can work well in the truth, but be catastrophic in error. The potential to overturn the work of God with false words is another motivation for them to guard their minds and thoughts and shield themselves with the Word and Spirit of God.

16. Prophetic obedience brings about their conscientious and meticulous sides. Over and over, prophets are driven to hear God, accurately interpret what He says or desires, and be scrupulous in following His commands. After a while, these practices end up cultivating sound qualities in them that turn out the pattern of godly behavior grown out of simple compliance with the will of the Lord.

Suggestion: Point out two examples of general prophetic obedience from the Bible.

Nature and Attributes of the Prophetic Anointing

To revive your appreciation for what the prophetic anointing is, and to refresh yourself on its value to this study, refer back to this subject's explanation under the Apostle's Office. The anointing you will remember, as discussed here, is addressing the **ministerial dispensation** the Lord gives those who stand in these offices, over what the Father imparts to His children upon adopting them into His family. The ministerial anointing is the heavier, denser concentrations of the Spirit that upgrade the natural abilities, enhance the minister's endowments, authorize and effectuate his service. It licenses and empowers his ministry acts.

The word for it, we discovered in the Greek, is *chrio*. It means to smear with oil, to consecrate to an office and/or religious service to furnish what is needed for its requirements. Below are the *chrio* descriptions of the prophet. Their importance is seen in their distinctions from the other offices and how they may be recognized as characteristic of what the office both calls for and manifests.

1.   Sensitivity to spiritual matters and an aptitude for handling supernatural details is primarily characteristic. The prophet is supernaturally focused and integrates its elements into the vast part of his ministry service. It may seem as though he is only ethereal, but the grounding of the wisdom of God, if applied, stabilizes h i m and centers his functions in biblical wholesomeness.

Suggestion: Scripturally and practically identify and outline ten spiritual matters and five supernatural details. From what you have learned so far, identify the aptitudes you see the prophet would need to handle them.

2.   Molded to both the spiritual and the supernatural, the prophet's attentions are given largely to difficulties originating there first. Before concluding a situation is the result of a natural circumstance, the prophet will seek causes in the higher realms. The prophet's eye peers into the invisible realms of God's creations easily and discernment helps him or her detect the influences that may be contributing to a predicament. Their interpretation ability further aids prophets' evaluations by providing them with the insight needed to comprehend its nature and apply God's remedies to it. The remedy may be prophetic and in the form of sage counseling, divine instruction, wise recommendations, and referrals for cures and relief. Mature prophets take seriously their impact and use prudence and discretion when administering God's truth to situations. They realize God's desire is that His flock be in soundness of mind, body, soul, and spirit.

Suggestion: Present a case for the above and then outline the prophet's ideal evaluation and application processes.

3.   Highly intuitive, perceptive, incisive instincts help the prophet probe the mysterious to open people's minds to the things of God. Through these, the prophet enables them to grasp the truths of His word and His kingdom. Keenness hones their capacity to identify affectations and to project the likely outcomes of what many find unimportant. Prophets, therefore, accentuate outcomes over image and motives over expressions.

Suggestion: Define and exemplify this category.

4.   Lyrical, poetic, theatrical, and musical sways dominate the prophet's ministrations. Their impartations reflect, over all, the temperaments and personalities of God. The prophet's actuations bring forth the peculiar views, perspectives, and position of God on the matters He chose to use the prophet to deal with. Their sensibilities are, if they are compelled by Him, especially acute to the feelings of the Lord and they are capable of articulating those feelings to others correctly to help them arrive at true conceptions of the Personhood of the Lord and His resemblance to their humanness. So you will often hear the prophet pointing out the emotions, hurts, pains, and sufferings of God by the hardheartedness of man. They will also rightly unveil the Lord's aspirations, desires, and needs concerning the Body on earth.

Suggestion: Study portions of the major prophets under these headings and extract incidences that substantiate the above.

5.   Especially attuned to the pleasure the Lord takes in high praise, prophets are intolerant of irreverence, erroneous, or carnal worship practices. They cannot abide disrespect for the Lord by His congregations and would generally not be caught indulging in practices and customs that belittle God's holiness or that instigate callousness toward Him. God's express exactions for approaching and fellowshipping with, or interacting with Him as a Body, is deeply etched in the prophet as a result of his training. Hence, the anointing can appear strict and its demands for godly worship rigid to the arrant believer who feels God is worthy of anything he chooses to offer him.

6.   Particularly interested in learning and teaching what the Lord deems for effective worship and responsible service, the prophet stresses (if he has submitted to it himself) the fruitful connection between knowledge and understanding, and mature godly service. The prophet combats sloppiness and irresponsibility in the things of God with training, education, and practical guidance. He generally does not subscribe to the "every man his own way" philosophy of the modern church. Jeremiah's words (9:24) say well what the prophet feels is responsible believer perspectives and pursuits. The prophet also does not take to or condone the spirit of independence and individuality pervading the Body today. For the prophet knows that unity, surrender, and harmony are the principal means of accomplishing this Christian walk.

7.   Prophets' abstract senses incline them to seeing visions, having spiritually significant dreams, making prophetic predictions, revealing Scripture, expounding on the Word, sensing the Holy Spirit, and discerning the times and the seasons of God's ordained events. Their mantle is appointed the transcendent currents of life and living which they pick up through these means.

8.   Knowledgeable of Scripture, prophets—in respect to human nature, sin, salvation, and their expressions and influences—keep their applications fresh and their relevance obvious to contemporary man generation after generation.

NOTE: For an analysis of the training of the prophet, see the text recommended throughout this book.

1. Discuss why prophets are, and must be, standoffish.

2. What is the detriment to the prophet who lacks his Christ identity?

3. The rough, tender exterior of the prophet explains what?

4. Prophet defiance speaks of what?

5. The prophet's mysterious side is valuable how?

6. High morality is critical to the prophet in what ways?

7. Explain the nature of the prophet's message in connection with his basic sincerity.

8. Teaching prophets are necessary for what reasons?

9. The prophet as a strategic warrior refers to what?

10. The prophet's responsiveness to the will and moods of God mean what?

11. Link the poetic, musical side of the prophet to your answer above?

12. Prophet objectivity and impartiality address what?

13. Prophet thinking resources applies to what?

14. Explain prophet obedience.

15. Prophet sensitivity and aptitude enable him to do what?

16.	The prophet's orientation to the spiritual and supernatural explain what about him?

17.	Relate the prophet's intuition and perception to #16 above.

18.	What sways dominate the prophet's ministrations? How and why?

19.	How is high praise instrumental to the prophet's ministry?

20.	Discuss the prophet's emphasis on knowledge and understanding and godly service.

21.	Describe the prophet's abstract senses.

22.	Discuss the prophet and the Scriptures.

CHAPTER SEVEN
The Evangelist

The Evangelist

Introduction

The office of the evangelist is next in our order due to his office also being itinerant. He is last in the line of primarily traveling ministers. His ministry is of prime importance. Research shows the evangelist to be the first point of contact between Christ and the sinner. He acts as the bridge between life and death and is the means whereby the dead cross over into salvation's eternal life. No other office has as its premier function and criterion of achievement the "giving of life to the dead" like the evangelist. His is a pivotal office. If the apostle's work starts in motion that which culminates into a full blown church or ministry, and the prophet that which restores to God, then the evangelist has as his distinctive the effect of delivering life to the dead. It has to be seen, on account of this, as equal in importance and esteem with the others.

Without the evangelist, the remainder of the officers would be out of business, or without a reason for answering their call to the ministry. Their would be no souls to apostle and thus no Body of saints from which to rear up prophets. No Body means no shepherd or pastor would be needed and no one would require discipleship teaching. There would be no Body for God and Christ to inhabit by the Spirit on earth. The effect of eliminating the evangelist would be the same as that of showing a video cassette in the reverse. When you touch the rewind button, here is what would take place.

First the Body would disappear, followed by the teacher and the pastor. Next the prophet would fade away and the apostle would go behind him. The ascension of Jesus Christ would be reversed, and the grave would back up to the cross. The Lord would come down from the cross and the trial and crucifixion of the Redeemer would unwind. The ministry and life of Christ would recede into the womb of the virgin who bore Him. The seed implanted in the woman would back up into the Godhead and the way of salvation would unravel as if it never happened and thus be unknown to man. Israel would still be under divine judgment, while the Gentiles would still not know the true and living God. All this would be the effect if the evangelist were suddenly wiped out of the ranks of the Ephesians 4:11 offices.

The evangelist is an officer of the church, just like the others. For the evangelist, however, the emphases are drastically different. Having no congregation to watch over, no covenanted ones to restore, no founding commission, and no disciples to teach, one could ask what does the evangelist have to officiate? The answer is plenty. The evangelist is the officiator of life—God's life—and eternal "zoe" life. They are the administrating executives of everlasting life to the world. The evangelist officiates the resurrection and restorative life brought by Jesus and imparted by the Holy Spirit. The office of the evangelist is the agency of regeneration. Their mandate is to "go and save souls." They are to relieve the vast human suffering by spreading the Christ life. Evangelists are sent to disciple the terrains of the dead and overturn the graveyards of sin. Their mandate is to cast down tombstones, revive the zombies, rob the graves and darkness of their treasures. Evangelists give the precious gift of eternal life to those who might hear and believe the Gospel of Jesus Christ, to those who want to live and not die. Jesus' teaching in John 5:24-30 relates it best. The evangelist is the officer of the church of Jesus Christ charged with this mission.

The Evangelist versus the Evangelizer

Like the gift of prophecy, the presence of the Holy Spirit given as a seal of salvation means all believers in Jesus can evangelize, and they should. In the same way the prophet and the gift of prophecy are unlike each other, the case is the same with the evangelist. Those who witness Jesus, as they say, are not by virtue of doing so, evangelists. The office is a permanent standing (until it is changed) but the act is intermittent. One is full time (tent-making notwithstanding); the other is sporadic. Witnessing, nonetheless effective, is the move of the Spirit for incidental use; the other is the mission mandated by the Lord Jesus.

As you can see, the station of an officer is miles beyond the operation of a gift. The question becomes then, what, in addition to life, sets the evangelist apart from the typical evangelizer? To understand this, you will need to go back to the front of this text and reread the section on the Officer's Foundations. Outside of the differentiations made there, the explanations and descriptions imparted to the officer have a charge, a mantle, empowerments and endowments. Also, authorities support and proliferate their output. Evangelists have the power gifts and supports that all the officers have, up to and including a discrete mission. Before we delve into the subject further to discuss the main factors that separate the two, the evangelist and the evangelizer, let us scour some scriptures that clue us in on the role, labors, and impacts of the office. The collection of scriptures that follow are called (for the purposes of this study) Evangelistic Scriptures. The first set comes from the Book of Isaiah.

While it is mainly a prophetic book, Isaiah presents some of the most concentrated passages on evangelism to be found in the Old Testament. It capsulizes wonderfully the spirit of the evangelist and the heart of God concerning it. The most passages pertaining to this subject are located in Isaiah chapters 49-61. A thorough study of them would enlighten even the newcomer to the field to the basics of the ministry: For example, Isaiah 49:1,2 show the ordinations of the Messiah; verses 3 and 4 give the call, and 5 and 6 give the mission. Verses 7-9 outline the Messiah's message and salvation. The word of salvation is seen in verses 20-21. Over in chapter 51, there is the history and origin of salvation, with 6b declaring its finality. Verse 8b gives its worth, and 9, its background. Isaiah 52:7 praises the Gospel of salvation as 8 shows its redemptive powers of unity and uniformity. Chapter 52:11 outlines its rescue, and the famous 53rd chapter discusses, at length, salvation's passion, the suffering of the Savior, and the sinfulness of the race He is to redeem by it. Isaiah 55 foretells the world's invitation to salvation and its provisions and blessings. The elements of salvation, chiefly repentance, are seen in 55:6,7, with verses 12 and 13 unveiling its delivering and restorative effects.

Admonishment and promise open Isaiah 56, and the expressions of salvation follow. The reasons for salvation are seen in 56:9-22. From here we move to Isaiah 59 where the Lord's charges and chastenings against the people are described, and chapter 60 begins the vision of salvation's completion. Chapter 61 is Luke 4:18's prophecy of the evangelism that leads to salvation for all and the promises awaiting those who partake of it. Isaiah 62 gives the view of salvation's success.

130

All these references set the stage for the ministry of the evangelist. To them we add Psalm 22, which predicts the cross of salvation and Psalm 85, which specifies the conditions and implications for salvation. Other worthwhile studies that help this examination include the Gospel Epilogues, studied in the beginning. Luke 4:18, referred to earlier, and Acts 15:6-11 set forth the message of the evangelist and the messenger himself. These too give further guidance and insight on the ministry and its emphases in respect to the evangelist, which Acts 21:8 tells us that Philip, one of the original deacons, was among the first. Acts 4:12 tops it all off: All *must* be saved.

The Office of the Evangelist

This is the Christian Ministry Invader's Office. Ordinarily the evangelist is the frontrunner of the Kingdom. Previous explanations say why. Theirs is a ministry of blazing a trail for the converts to Jesus Christ to repent and come into His Body. For this reason, the apostolic anointing, according to Paul, requires a good amount of evangelism to found and expand its work.

The evangelist gleans for souls by preaching a distinct message: the message of the Cross, which they know is the Gospel of Salvation (the good. news) and the Gospel of Jesus Christ (the word of truth). The Gospel as the word of truth concerning the Savior centers on His mission and message. It includes His incarnation, His crucifixion, resurrection and ascension. Its essences points up the sin nature of man and the means God ordained to remedy it. Grace and faith (Ephesians 2:8) are the source of evangelistic authority.

The Gospels' historical foundation comes from the Old Testament. Jesus authorized (canonized) them during His ministry on the earth. Specifically, He authenticated in Luke 24:44, the Law of Moses, the Prophets, and the Psalms. In quoting and referring to Solomon, the Lord authorized the Proverbs. His references to David, Solomon, and the Kings, or events occurring in their times, canonized the Kings and the Chronicles. Ruth was included in the Lord's lineage. Ecclesiastes and Song of Solomon were other products of the king's wisdom. Job prefigures the Messiah and uncovers the Almighty's creatorship. Ezra and Nehemiah record the fulfillment of prophecies uttered by both Isaiah and Jeremiah, prophets of God. Hadassah's rise to Esther the queen shows divine providence in that her position enabled her to save the nation of Israel from certain annihilation to fulfill the Abrahamic Covenant. On the basis of this, her acts deserved to be part of the Scripture's canonization. Joshua's completion of Moses' mission as his preordained successor validates his book's inclusion in the divine record. Judges is recognized on the strength of Samuel's ministry as the Judge in Israel. He was recalled by God in His words to the Prophets. The book of Hebrews mentions him along with Gideon, David, Jephthah, David, and Samuel. His service bridges Joshua with the account of the prophet's services. Furthermore, the book's chronicles of the various tribes' activities and failures additionally canonizes its place in the register of God's history of redemption. The epistles writer's eyewitness of Christ and His ministry (and teachings) canonized them. Revelation was authenticated by one of the twelve.

For the evangelist, understanding the biblical supports that substantiate his message and ministry is important. Knowing what authenticates his teachings and witness, and what authorizes his invasion of the kingdom of darkness, is imperative. Evangelists know salvation, repentance, the new birth, the sinner's prayer, and their results more intricately than others. Ideally, the God appointed evangelist knows it is the Scriptures uttered and inspired by Christ that will get the job done; therefore, thorough Scripture study is imperative to the evangelist's training. They realize, on the basis of this training, that the power is found in God's word, His truth, and the testimonial record He gave us of Himself and His Son.   The ideal of the message of the cross is the Lord's fulfillment of what was started way back in the Garden of Eden. His summons of Abram, rescue of Moses, inauguration of David, protection of the nation, and appointment of the prophets all reflect the thread of salvation running through the incarnation of the Son throughout history.   Just as God drew the lost to His Son, evangelists are the people specially made to draw lost souls to them by the Spirit of the Son within. Both Peter's and Paul's sermon records confirm this.

The work record goes on and continues until the Revelation of Jesus given to John. It recalls the abuse of His prophets over the centuries. The recount of the slaughter of the apostles and disclosure of the presence of the same spirit of Jezebel that plunged natural Israel into the depths of Satanism lends credibility to its inclusion in the Word of the Lord. Every book of the Bible, every record of Scripture, every prophecy, revelation, and ministry contained in it is important to the evangelist's ministry. These serve as the premise for the power they wield and the results they achieve. When he or she stands in the fullness of this office there is no one who can better breakthrough the holds of sin and darkness on an unbeliever to seize a soul for Christ than the evangelist.

The information given above was outlined to enlighten you on the evangelist as a life giver and to stress the importance of his ministry and message and show how he comes by his particular anointing. The following examination of the word *evangelist* will better help you to see the rightness of the "life giver" application to the mission and force of the evangelist's ministry.

The Greek primary root of the word is *eu*, which means "good or well." From this comes the prefix for the words *life* or *live*. In our language, we translate the *eu* to *ev* as in Eve. It is used somewhat interchangeably. The remainder of the word "evangelist" addresses its messenger aspect. Thus, the evangelist is a good messenger of well-being and life, or a messenger of life filled with well-being. Think on this for a moment. The explanation is telling you something extremely important. It is saying that the very words coming out of the mouth and being of the evangelist give life. They literally inject it into the being of the hearer. What is meant here is that something within the evangelist is potent enough to reverse death. It is that something that serves as the basis for his or her mandate: *to spread life*.   The labors of evangelists, therefore, cause people to live by reviving them. Not only that, their words implant what is needed to keep them from death and leave them with the gift of eternal and everlasting life.

Explanations given above take our traditional view of the evangelist and broaden it greatly. He is more than a preacher who travels about. For the evangelist, these are all mediums by which he spreads what is in him: the good word of life. Oh, but there is more. The evangelist's message leaves the revived—the saved—with the promise of additional life and the preservation of the new life they have received. Contained within that life are the properties of recovery, reparation, and restoration, as well as a legal contract bringing the convert into covenant with God—the very things the evangelist was enlisted for. They are all the virtues that accompany the officer in the executions of his office.

The word of life spoken by him integrates healing, deliverance, rescue, and special provisions of ministration besides. The evangelist, by the grace of God within him, knows instinctively the blend of spiritual words that make him successful, that follow up his activities with evidence (See Philip's fruit in Acts 8:5-14). Philip preached Christ. Simply put, he told them about the Messiah, all those things we spelled out previously. His words ignited faith, generated miracles, drove out demons, and healed and delivered many. Philip confronted occultism and overturned its hold in the city, taking the top sorcerer down in the process. This was one evangelist, mind you!

Suggestion: Relate how the word's etymology broadens the traditional view of the evangelist as you see it now.

From these references you can witness the gift of eternal life manifested itself in an improved, natural life. Why? Because of the invigorating words buried in the spirit and soul of the evangelist. The Gospel—the good news of truth, the message of life by that truth preached—breaks the holds that allow people to believe and thus repent to receive the Agent of the Godhead standing by to gain legal entry into the vessel, once guarded by the devil.

Picking up on the Hebrew roots of the word "evangelist," it gives us the word *chavah*, translated "Eve, giver of life." It means to cause to live by declaration, or to show one alive (or how to live) by declaration. This term is related to the Hebrew *chayah*. The word for life used to describe what Elisha's bones did to the corpse that fell on them is this very word. The residual life contained in them caused it to return to life. The precise affect is what the words of the evangelist have on those who hear and believe the word of God from him. *Chayah* means "to give life, to quicken, to generate recovery and restoration." Not only are the converts of the evangelist's ministry saved (preserved), they are made whole, invigorated, repaired, and left with a promissory token to be kept in that state by the Lord's Spirit within. Study Ephesians 1 and extract from its teachings that which pertains to the above.

The most interesting thing about the word "evangelist" is that its meaning includes the name for the first woman Eve. We alluded to this earlier. It tells us that the action of the evangelist is spiritually likened to Eve's role in natural procreation. She conceived seed, she incubated the babe, she travailed, and she gave birth. The evangelist, figuratively, does the same for the sons and daughters born to God. This aspect of his move explains the cross reference research that the word led us to. Combined, they speak of another work of the office, that of gathering out of one assembly to place in the assembly of another. It implies competing for the souls of darkness, of contending for them, inferring that conflicts arise as a consequence of the labors. These we know are spiritual and refer to the demons holding sway over the lives of those God called to salvation.   One word, *ago*, denotes the leading out, driving out, or inducing to leave (the world for instance) to enter Christ.

Suggestion: Research the epistles for biblical examples of the above paragraph.

The word suggests the birthing process that opens the way for the exit from sin and the entrance to life. The evangelist, unknown to many, struggles in prayer and wrestles with the hosts of darkness and unbelief to herd the lost into the fold of Christ. To do this they must powerfully drive out the enemy binding them and lead the redeemed away from that which enslaved them in the yoke of sin. This calls for not only preaching the message of conversion, but for steering the convert into the church that will teach and care for him; a church that will nurture him and rear him up in the Lord.

What gives the evangelist his official status is the prefix of the word that defines his ministry as a manner of life. That speaks to profession. The position's listing among the five-fold ranks it with the others and thereby accredits its dispensation with the same authoritative features the others have. Although evangelists do not have a church or a study following, so to speak, they do have staffs, workers, supporters, and such. Over these they have authority. In addition, the evangelist's field being the world gives all of them extraordinary supernatural powers to meet and tackle the strongmen of the spirit world who refuse to release those who seek deliverance and salvation. Here their authority is infinitely more pronounced.

Chapter Seven Review 1

1.   The evangelist is third in rank for what reason?

2.   Summarize the effect of removing the evangelist from the scene.

3.   How is the evangelist, too, an officer?

4.   Distinguish the evangelist from the evangelizer.

5.   Review the Evangelistic Scriptures and their importance to the ministry.

6.   Why and how is the evangelist an invader's office?

7.   Overview the canonization of the Scriptures.

8.   *Eu* means what?

9.   #8 is related to the evangelist how?

10.   Explain the evangelist as a life giver.

11.   Define *chavah* and *chayah*. Connect their meanings with the evangelist.

12.   Explain the similarity between the evangelist and Eve.

13.   Discuss what gives the evangelist his official status.

14.   Overview the nature of evangelistic authority.

Features of the Evangelist's Office

Regularly, we see traditionalists attach the title of evangelist to different ministers. Often it is as if the office is seen as a "catchall" for anyone who does not know his place in the ministry. As far as women are concerned, the title of evangelist is the only one many churches will allow them to have. Not a proponent of women in ministry, the office least respected, the evangelist, is the one biased, sexist churches slot any female who displays any sort of preaching ability or official ministerial capacity outside of the Sunday School teacher. This is most unfortunate as it causes those who are truly called to the office to be reluctant to stand in it because of the "it's women's work" connotation attached to it. Others won't embrace the call because they see the evangelist as only a visiting missionary who takes food to the hospital or the hungry and says feeble prayers over the oppressed.

We have shown that neither of these contentions are true. The evangelist is not a scoop office to stash uncertain, indecisive, or would be ministers of the church in. It is not an office of pacification to bestow to placate what may be considered pushy women. Neither is the evangelist's office the burial ground for mediocre ministry. The evangelist is a powerful, vital minister whose efforts see that the church continues to exist generation after generation. It has both necessity and credibility and should not be clogged with inept, indifferent, and position-hungry figureheads whose ministry concept is white outfitted convocations and draping front row church seats waiting until an available Sunday arrives to preach to the saints. This perception can be faulted for declining church membership, widespread. unbelief and callousness, and innumerable souls lost to hell.

The evangelist has definite purpose. He is a first line introduction to the Lord Jesus Christ and an underground warrior to snatch souls out of the clutches of sin. The evangelist is unemployed until his next meeting, conversion, or sermon. His is the ministry that ever has to be on the road winning souls to Christ, and preparing others to do the same. The evangelist will knock on doors, face and challenge strangers, and travel the highways and hedges compelling the souls to come into the kingdom. The official evangelist will interact with the churches to flood the community with the message of Christ, and will offer himself to be engaged to see that new converts are always added to the Body, and thus the churches.

Like the prophet, the evangelist may be in fellowship with several churches at once. He may cover a circuit ministering in and on behalf of each one regularly to aid their evangelistic outreach efforts. Ideally, these churches will support his work, and he will maintain right relationship with them to keep the doors of outreach open in their neighborhoods. Innovative approaches to reaching every strata of life for Christ are needed by the evangelist: One thing he is not called to do is pad the membership of any one Body or to confine his labors to one lone church. For the most part, the evangelist is on God's schedule and should be ready to be dispatched to His designated fields at a moment's notice.

Full time evangelists need to be alert to opportunities to establish routine meetings held at regular intervals. If churches are not willing to accommodate them, then community houses, neighborhood centers, even the home of supportive saints are good locations for scheduling and holding frequent soul winning meetings.

The Evangelist's Anointing

l. The evangelist's particular burden is the reality of hell and the lost soul's obligation to it. It is not unusual for the evangelist to have had visions of hell, recurrent dreams of what goes in hell, and strange insight into the agonies that await a soul's entrance into hell. Their characteristic fiery sermonizing is largely due to these experiences and visitations from the demons of the underworld as proof of eternal judgment.

2. Evangelists are especially grieved by hurting and suffering people, most specifically *lost* hurting and suffering people. For an evangelist, a deathbed conversion is priceless. They are the ones to visit the sick to assure they are in right stead with the Lord and who stand on the street corner impelling sinners to repent and be saved.

3. Evangelists are fiery, fervent, emotionally charged people whose personality is specially suited to arousing the passions and emotions of a sinner. Conversations with them are rousing and dynamic. Their affection for the Savior and peculiar apprehension of what it cost Him to make the way of salvation are high motivators for those genuinely called to the office. Indifference toward sin and casualness about getting souls into the kingdom are not signs of the true evangelist.

4. Evangelists can teach, that is impart God's truth in a lecture setting, but the strength of their ministry is best seen in preaching. Captives of the faculties bestowed upon them, their witnessing to communicate the express message of the Gospel is provocative and arresting. For them the work of Christ, the cross of Calvary, Pentecost, and the baptism of the Holy Spirit have consequential significance—a significance that moves them to venture into the unknown, and even the unsafe, to spread the word of salvation. Their mandate drives them to obey their last vision of a lost soul. They follow the Holy Spirit's leadership to the place where they can share Christ and pilot them to salvation.

5. The evangelist's anointing is characterized by strong demonstrations of the Spirit of God. Their ministry is likely to exhibit miracles, signs, and wonders. They are given to working deliverance miracles, healings, and signs to persuade a sinner of the reality of hell, his or her eternal destination, and the power of Christ to save him or her from sin. The gift of prophecy often attends their ministry, and the manifestations of the Spirit's power and revelation demonstrations frequently under gird their ministrations.

6. For the evangelist, the message and the options are clear. Heaven or hell, salvation or sin, the Savior or Satan. This is different from the thrust of the Apostolic and Prophetic message, which centers on (once salvation is established) holiness or hell, sanctification or destruction, righteousness and godliness in character expressions, and maturity and growth in the kingdom of God. The former two relentlessly attack and ward off apostasy. Evangelists' prime aim is to get the sinner into eternal life. They are not especially concerned with their nurturing or knowledge. These are concerns of the pastor who receives them from the delivery table of conversion.

7. Evangelists have a curious appreciation of the place of God's love in soul winning. They know the sinner understands his condemned state, so they focus on the love that sent forth His Son to die for the salvation of the world. Nevertheless, the true evangelist

knows that there can be no genuine conversion where there is no repentance. Therefore the call to repent, trumpeted by Jesus in the beginning, has prominent place in their message.

8. The evangelist's office is enhanced by its missionary spirit. Evangelists are called to seek and to save that which was lost. They are to go out into all the world to preach the Gospel. They are to set their tables to invite the maimed, the lame, and the crippled to come to the supper of the Lord. The evangelist without an established plan to evangelize and a program of evangelism is not an evangelist, but rather an occasional evangelizer. The world, not the church, is the territory of the evangelist.

Personality of the Evangelist

1. Energetic, fervent, and driven by the burden of the lost, no matter what state they are in, is the heart of the evangelist. The evangelist has a heavy burden for those who do not know Christ. He or she travails inwardly at the sight of them. The evangelistic burden unexpectedly catches him up in weeping and wailing, tears and groans of travail for the spiritual breakthroughs needed to release a lost soul to salvation. His commitment to his call causes him to be a ready vessel of strenuous intercession.

2. They are bold, courageous, and dedicated, as well as forceful. Taking all kinds of risks, evangelists can't help but fearlessly walk up to strangers and ask them if they know Jesus. After their name almost, the evangelist wants to know the eternal state of everyone they encounter. Evangelists are not easily intimidated and appear reckless in their cause for Christ. They are some of the most persuaded people you will meet whose fervor and affection do not stop with words. They seize every opportunity to put in action what they believe in their hearts.

3. Evangelists are sensitive, fiery personalities. They tend to be highly emotional because of the need to persuade souls of the sincerity of their message enough to repent and convert. Their instincts sense the salvation timing of those they minister to, making them sound authoritarian in their exhortation to the wavering sinner to get saved. Persistent, once aroused by the unsaved state of someone in their presence, the evangelist can bear down heavily in the spirit and in the natural on the forces holding sinners back from conversion.

4. Evangelists can be both dutiful and somewhat studious, although, sad to say, far too many evangelists reject formalized training in favor of personal interpretation of the word of God because of church's disdain for the office. Hence the office is often fraught with erroneous messages, haphazard service, and immature ministers. This is why more evangelists do not have more powerful demonstrations of the Spirit. Since the degree of anointing is in direct proportion to the knowledge, wisdom, and prudence the minister displays, lack of training hampers many of their ministries. Those who apply themselves to learn and be accurate in their dispensation will find the intensity of their gift increasing comparably. Their effort toward knowledge and integrity shows their determination to bring glory to the Lord and His truth, as God's Spirit, they know, simply cannot confirm a lie.

5. Evangelists are outgoing, personable, and people-oriented. Due to the requirements of their ministry, evangelists are naturally sociable people. A warm, engaging personality is a must for them to strike up the conversations needed to share Christ. With almost enviable ease, they open the lines of communication with strangers to get in with people many find difficult or unpleasant. Evangelists are not quickly put off by rejection. Most of them have a sound understanding of how the devil strategically uses offensiveness as a weapon against salvation and don't allow their emotions to get in the way of duty. You will rarely find an evangelist, or any ordained officer for that matter, too offended or upset by the sinner's responses to his overtures to complete the ministering it takes to open the door to salvation and deliverance.

6. Evangelists are compassionate and merciful. While they are strong and determined when it comes to their service, they do not lose sight of the fragility of those they must take under their wing. Many evangelists have stalwart temperaments that are not recoiled at the condition they may find a soul in because of his sin. The unpleasantness that wreaks from a body in distress is another thing that will not distract them from what they are called to do. They overlook the odor of the alcoholic, the uncleanness of the homeless, and the smell of wasting away the diseased might have. The evangelist will do the chores others would run from to prove to the sufferer the love of Christ and that their own expression of it is real. By this they often relax the defensive guards sufferers have put up against insult and neglect in order to get them to hear the Gospel and lead them to salvation. Evangelists are motivated by the fact that they cannot stand to witness human suffering idly, or see people bound and lost in their sin.

The Nature of the Office

1.   Dynamic, itinerant
2.   Miraculous and highly charged
3.   Confrontational and warring
4.   Outreach oriented and global minded
5.   Militant and combatant
6.   Has preaching emphases
7.   Should be field headquartered
8.   Requires local affiliation and interaction
9.   Needs regular circuit for consistency
10. Must have strong inter-community activities
11. Involves extensive intercession and travail
12. Should seek refinement training for increased effectiveness
13. Is suffocated by lone church affiliation and service
14. Has official status and authority
15. Should not be treated lightly or misused to appease church bias or disrespect.

Evangelism versus Revival

Evangelism and revival are not the same thing. Unfortunately, people hold revivals as though they were outreach services. It is true the evangelist's mandate is to spread life;

however, the target audience of their ministry is not the apathetic or apostate saved, but the unregenerate lost. Somehow pastors think that they will increase their church rosters by having evangelists come in to "revive" their congregants. What having the evangelists come in will do is to provide an opportunity for those who are unsaved and hiding out in the pew to hear the Gospel, repent, and get born again. For this reason, having them minister from time to time to catch up those who may not have had the right slant of the message preached to them for conviction is an excellent idea. To have evangelists come in and hold revivals to rejuvenate stagnant congregants is simply not scriptural. Evangelists are world oriented. They are sent to evangelize, that is **to bring the good new of Christ's salvation to the world**. A revival is a different thing entirely. Its purpose is to revive; to bring to life again. It is to fire up those who have fallen asleep in their flesh or become spiritually dull in the things of God. For this the church needs teachers who impart fresh truth or remind them persuasively of why they got saved and joined the church in the first place.

Study Josiah, Hezekiah, Jehoshaphat, and Asa's ministries. These are four kings who are credited with some of the most revolutionary reforms in Israel's history. What you will find out is that they accomplished this through teaching, not preaching the salvation message anew. Teachers are more anointed to accomplish revivals than evangelists for this reason. Often a prophet with a teaching anointing is more effective than the most powerful preaching of evangelists. One reason is the evangelist, no matter how he tries, inevitably ends up bringing the message of the cross and the subject of salvation into his sermons in some way or another. While there is certainly no harm in this, the problem with it is that it does not apply to those saved already. That means they will eventually get tired of the same circle of messages and become restless because their spirit is not being fed. In the same way a natural baby desires heavier and stronger food, the spiritual man does also.

One distinguishing feature of a church pastored by an evangelist is that the members remain infantile in comparison with those shepherded by an ordained shepherd. The reason has to do with the faculties designed and supplied each officer and the incompatibility of those faculties with the anointing dispensed to them for the work God called them to do. An evangelist's anointing, for example, is for those who do not know Christ, who are completely ignorant to the church and spiritual matters. What they need are the basics that will help them make up their mind to receive salvation. The older Christian, on the other hand, understands (or can quickly understand because of the light in him) the basics that led him to get saved. What they need to know is what is next. Now that they are saved, most of them ask, "Now what?"

The evangelist's faculties, like all the other officers, attract the properties of the anointing that energize and empower him. If those faculties are those of a pastor, for instance, regardless of what they are, the requirements of that office will continually escape him.   If   he   pays attention to the pastors he deals with, he will notice they are focusing on things he has never even thought of. The pastor's understanding matches his call so he can see and discern things the evangelist would overlook or not see the importance of.   **And so it is with all the officers and every gift and anointing the Lord dispenses**. What the person is naturally endowed to do, aware of it or not, that is what his anointing will hook up with because the properties of the anointing are intelligent and will adhere to what they were dispensed for. A singer's anointing will not cohere with the vocal cords of one who has not the gift for singing.

It would simply be a waste since the absence of the gift signals the absence of the faculty, intelligence, and subsequently, the aptitude. This is so in addition to the absence of divine purpose.

Herein lays the difficulty of officers switching and swapping their calls. In addition to the anointing, the officers have mandates, missions, and ministry covenants that God will honor or ignore depending upon their compliance with His ordinations.

1. State the common traditionalist's view and treatment of the evangelist and how and why it came to be.

2. The evangelist as a first line warrior means what?

3. Lone evangelists have many problems. What are some of them?

4. What should full time evangelists do?

5. Describe the evangelist's burden.

6. What especially grieves evangelists?

7. Discuss the evangelist's mentality and its expressions.

8. Talk about evangelists and teaching.

9. What characterizes the evangelist's anointing? Illustrate.

10. Overview and explain the merits of the evangelist's message.

11. What do evangelists appreciate most?

12. What is the evangelist's office enhanced by?

13. What burden drives the evangelist? How and why?

14. Describe evangelists' boldness.

15. Discuss the knowledge drawback of the evangelists and its hazards and consequences in service.

16. Show how and why evangelists are naturally people oriented.

17. Comment on evangelists' compassion and mercy.

Bonus 1

Define and illustrate the 15 points of the evangelist's office.

Bonus 2

Explain, cite examples, and show the problem with evangelists running revivals.

Field Projects:

Write out a 25 point questionnaire using the material given in this section and plan how you would use it to enroll students in your upcoming evangelist course. *[To be presented]*

CHAPTER EIGHT
The Pastor

The Pastor

Introduction

The office of the Pastor is fourth in our study. It is not fourth because of its lesser importance, but because of where it enters the picture in the scheme of God's plan. The pastor ends the line of itinerant ministers and begins the order of stationary officers. Apostles break ground; prophets usually follow (or accompany) them to teach and to inform the church of God's present truth, in relation to it and the move the apostle has spearheaded. Evangelists, (either as the apostle's work of evangelism or the officer himself), generally precede the other three. All of them—the apostle, the prophet, and the evangelist—are the itinerant ministers of the Body. Theirs is a traveling ministry. The apostle is the one likely to remain still for the longest period of time of the three. The last two offices are stationary, the pastor more so than the teacher. The two, especially the pastor, nurture and edify the souls to be placed in the church.

The Pastor's office is the mainstay that stabilizes the fold. His is the bedrock of the offices. His principal duty is to keep the flock of God. The pastor is the Lord's resident caregiver, the stationary one who nestles down to virtually live with the sheep.

What a Pastor Is

The word "pastor" comes from the Hebrew *roei* and the Greek *poimen*. Both terms signify a shepherd: one who tends a flock of sheep. Aside from the pastor being a member of the officials of the church, he is a literal companion to his flock. The pastor becomes their partner in the Christian life, and a friend to guide them through their Christian walk. His chief responsibility is to feed, pasture, guide, tend, and overall care for his flock. He is to look upon them with patience and tenderness and take pleasure in his call to nourish them for the Lord.

By flock, both definitions mean, spiritually, a body of believers. The pastor's authority extends to being the presiding officer over the local congregation. He is to see to the management of its affairs and the direction of its activities as a godly community. His keeping of the sheep is to include ruling, government, supervision, and intimate association with the flock. The pastor's officiations involve church sacraments (baptism, communion, marriage, and funerals), teaching—especially of the virtues of the Christian faith, its tenets and doctrine—and continual impartation of the wisdom of the Lord to His flock. As a shepherd he is to find and maintain suitable pasture for the sheep and be watchful over their moral and spiritual conduct.

In shepherding, he is to provide for the needs of his flock to see they lack nothing God's covenant has made provisions for. As a pastor he is to see the sheep have appropriate accommodation for grazing, nurturing, growth, protection, and safety. As a leader, the shepherd is to steer them to the safe, righteous, godly and holy path of the Christian life. As a companion he is to be the helpmeet, comforter, consoler of the flock and a defense against any endangerment to their security. The anointed shepherd provides care and tending; supplies what he has been given from the Lord to his sheep; and reflects God's constancy and goodness by enabling the sheep to one day dwell with God. Moreover, he is to make every effort to see the sheep do not loiter, wander off the path of righteousness, or strain to return to their captivity.

Marks of the true shepherd are the following:

Concern for the sheep	Diligence in service
Dutiful vigilance	Sheep gathering
Perseverance	Rescue of lost and bound
Return of the rescued	Holy nurturing
Godly nourishment	Adequate pasturing
Conscientious preservation	Faithful care
Provide proper spiritual rest	Search for strays
Healing	Reparation
Mending	Defend threatened, vulnerable
Singleness of service	Devotion to flock, God
Attentiveness	Sacrifice
Promotion, release of blessings	Provisions of covenant
Enable abundant life	Establishment of safety
Enable liberation	Enable joy of freedom
Furnish security	Release enslaved possessions
Enrich redemption	Foster godly satisfaction

Suggestion: Detail the most significant things the above features may demonstrate to help one recognize the godly pastor.

By contrast, the hireling may be recognized. The hireling is the shepherd the Lord Jesus warned us about. He is the one who is only in it for the money; and merchandising the commodities of the God's kingdom is his chief aim.

Only looking at the opposites of the above will give you a good idea of what the Lord says is an ungodly pastor; however, there are several discrete things that readily expose him. They are the following characteristics:

Feed self and not the flock	Neglectful
Self indulgent	Abandon flock
Gluttonous, insatiable	Oblivious to flock suffering
Derelict	Selfish
Indifferent to flock needs	Insensitive to God, church
Cruel	
Reckless endangerment of flock	
Take the best of gifts to God	
Extraordinarily extravagant	

Suggestion: Compile a profile of the possible actions of the hireling.

The Shepherd's Life with His Sheep

The godly shepherd understands his role by exploring, observing, and imitating on the spiritual plane the pastoral life from which his office was patterned. God's choice of the word had strong meaning to Him. Of all the titles and expressions He could have chosen, the Lord selected the word "pastorate" to format the care and keeping of His sheep. The reasons are numerous, but fundamental to them is the nature of the sheep and His appreciation of their nature in relation to His own. Following are just a few explanations of the shepherd's life with his sheep.

1. Shepherds, to assure the safety of their flock, take pains to search out and select the most suitable place for the sheep to pasture. He considers elements, environments, geography, and supply. In addition to these, the shepherd must concern himself with the possibility of harm and danger coming upon him and his flock. Therefore, he seeks to locate a spot where there is minimum risk to the sheep and little exposure to the climate. Also, there is the matter of rights of access. For these the shepherd covenants with the local authorities for use of land that may belong to another to avert conflicts that can arise.

Suggestion: Explain what this is saying in modern terms and how it may be practiced today.

2. The shepherd's cloak is an important article of his clothing. It is a covering as well as a resource. The shepherd not only uses it for warmth, but doubles it as a bassinet for newborn sheep to secure and protect them during their travels over rough terrain. The cloak also serves as a hospice for ill, injured, and fragile little ones to ease their suffering and speed up their recovery.

Suggestion: Explain how a shepherd's cloak would be recognized and applied today in spiritual contexts.

3. The shepherd's rod is specially chosen and prepared as an emblem of his power and a weapon of defense. The word rod, synonymous with scepter, is to rule and to lead. The rod is used to club intruders who threaten the sheep and is accompanied by a staff as Psalm 23 indicates. The staff is a support and an instrument of discipline. It holds the shepherd steady as he climbs the rocks and brings a dawdling sheep back to the fold by the hook that is usually at the end. The rod defends while the staff supports.

Suggestion: Come up with three modern day examples and applications of this.

4. The shepherd's sling could be seen as a primitive projectile of defense against stalkers of the flock. It was effective in stopping human and animal predators, and alerting sluggish sheep to the presence of danger to prod him to catch up with the flock.

Suggestion: Detail what the contemporary shepherd's sling would be.

5.   The shepherd's close and constant presence is the essence of the management of his flock. Absent, he cannot effectively govern them, failing to be an eyewitness to their needs and the dangers lurking around them. Secondhand reporting can only provide the shepherd with unreliable information that may or may not be viewed as significant to him. The true shepherd is always with his sheep. Their constant exposure to the elements, terrain, animals, and robbers demand this if he is to fulfill his purpose for leading them. To offset the sheep's natural vulnerability to these hazards, the shepherd trusts no one to guard and keep his sheep for him. The shepherd's other concern is for the quality of the flock's pasture and feeding, that both are proper for their nourishment and safety.

Suggestion: Name three possibilities that would endanger spiritual sheep and the best means of averting or remedying it.

6.   One key to the shepherd's success is the sheep's obedience. They must follow him to enjoy his benefits and provisions. He must remain with them to assure their well being and security. Natural sheep panic when they lose sight of or no longer feel the presence of the shepherd. A stranger also alarms them as his unfamiliarity signals danger to them. To keep the sheep calm, the shepherd must regularly let them hear his voice. His sound to them is peculiar, unique, and reassuring. It cannot be imitated, and hearing it regularly comforts and consoles the flock. Unfamiliar or imitated sounds cause the sheep to scatter.

Suggestion: Explain this in modern day settings.

7.   The shepherd never leaves his fold. His perpetual presence is how he cares for the sheep and guarantees he is always nearby to safeguard them. The shepherd conscientiously obtains the best pasture and resting place for his sheep in the most expedient manner, so as not to prolong, unduly, their discomfort from the surroundings. The shepherd further entertains the sheep with music from his handmade flute. His music draws the younger sheep near quickly and soothes the older ones.

8.   The God-ordained shepherd, in every possible way, abides with his flock. His comprehension of the dangers waiting for them coupled with their innate exposure to attack, enslavement, and ravaging from hostile, cunning predators leads him to take precautions in his oversight of the flock. He knows sheep are naturally defenseless and are unaware of the real existence of danger. They also, when threatened, do not instinctively know what to do. Goats, on the other hand, likely members of the flock, unite to defend themselves against an adversary. Sheep scatter and make themselves an even easier prey. Being knowledgeable of all this, the shepherd will stand by to avert these crises and to personally bring and guide his sheep out and in. He personally endeavors to safely bed them down at night.

9.   The shepherd leads his sheep through the currents of life for pasturing, for nourishment, for provisions and security. When one stumbles and falls, he is there to pick him up or to break the fall. His senses alert him to the imminent peril waiting for any one of them.

Suggestion: Explicate how this would be accomplished today by Christ's shepherd and under what specific conditions.

10.   The shepherd knows his sheep. He knows them as a group and intuitively comprehends their makeup as a flock. The shepherd, though his is never away from his sheep, does not find the responsibility for them burdensome because they interest him.. He is fond of each one and is inspired to give some pet names that characterize their uniqueness and special traits. A habit, a pleasure, a behavior, or a feat may lead the shepherd to call a sheep by a pet name to express the particular warmth and intimacy he shares with some. The names the shepherd chooses invariably signify some unusual delight a sheep may bring him or some ability or practice he finds especially impressive. The sheep do not bore the shepherd, though they may present him with many challenges; yet he finds them fascinating and their separate personalities needful.

11. Jesus' dispatch of the twelve in pairs signifies the heart of he shepherd and his deep concern for their security and safety. The shepherd knows the devastation of aloneness, and understands the basic weakness of his flock. Pairing them off keeps them from isolation and thus the threat of loneliness. True sheep easily fall into the pattern. The shepherd gets so accustomed to the pairs he recognizes that he quickly spots the absence of one. He can tell by the mere appearance of the flock when the composition is charged and one is missing. Jesus' parable of the 99 is based on this system of numeration. An even number is the standard, and the wandering away of one leaves an imbalanced 99, which is difficult to overlook. The lone sheep will reflect the loss of his partner having to travel with the flock unescorted.

12. Intimacy between the shepherd and sheep is so great that the shepherd, without seeing, can identify his sheep. What is placed in his heart for each one will tell him who is, or who is not, his own. The same is true with the sheep. They do not need to be introduced to their shepherd more than once. Upon introduction, the shepherd embraces the sheep and the sheep depends upon the shepherd for the duration of their union.

The Sheep of the Flock

Though flocks intermingle, no sheep will join himself to another flock. The voice of another shepherd frightens, not attracts, them. Their security is upset when they are separated from the one who has cared for and led them along the way. Sheep are helpless, completely without support or defense, without a shepherd. Throughout Scripture it is not noted once that God ever left His sheep without a shepherd. They may wander, but the Lord designates a shepherd to watch over and supply every one of them.

Sheep need moral foundations and biblical moorings for the Christian life that God has deposited in His shepherds to give them. Without them, the sheep turn to, and in on, themselves. They conceal what needs to be repented of, and they dally and err with no definite guidance or anointed dispensation to direct them. They need to be prodded, scolded, corrected, strengthened, and stretched in the things of God. The losses, trials, and sorrows of life, common to man, furthermore overrun them. The predators of darkness stalk them like an unattended child defenseless without his guardian.

An unsubmitted will makes shepherdless sheep easy prey to real dangers. Also, they become prone to anxiety or imagined harm over unfounded threatenings. Evil beckons them to the wilderness, dressed up as Christian maturity, godly wisdom, and "take care of myself" motivation. Once lured into the wilderness of sin and destruction, unattended sheep are seduced and slaughtered by the very inducement that ensnared them. The absence of a shepherd leaves no one to admonish them against flirting with danger or to warn then of true harm. Besides, the absence of a shepherd means no one is deliberately praying for their safety and welfare.

Without a shepherd, sheep's natural mute surrender to "come what may" causes them to resign themselves to the hopelessness and doom of life put upon them by satanic forces. Some of these surrenders are needless, and unnecessarily tie yokes of bondage about the sheep's necks.

The Intrinsics of the Pastor's Being

As the natural shepherd has buried within himself, on his person, all that is needed to tend and nurture his flock, so too does the spiritual shepherd. His being is the reservoir of his personal resources, containing the wisdom he needs to employ and to apply. Love, friendship, delight, and desire characterize the shepherd's want for his sheep. These keep his heart toward them. No matter the size of the flock, the shepherd can discern the cry of his sheep and recognize which one is in trouble. When it comes to approaching danger, his instincts reveal the direction in which it is coming along with the cause and its solution.

Even if his congregation is a large one, a traumatic or dramatic event will be made known to him concerning his flock in a vision, a dream, or similar form of revelation. He may see it in advance or detect it in the presence of the one to be affected or afflicted. In either case, the shepherd will sense the coming of harm against his sheep if he is alert, prayerful, and not overwhelmed with the cares of this life.

Pastors of large churches, in the development of serious incidences, may see a face in prayer or while asleep, an outfit, or a distinguishing mark. They may hear a voice or note a mannerism to accompany a revelatory warning or communication. Upon encountering the one to whom it pertains, there may be a quickening flashback to recall the earlier message to the pastor and inform him on the attention he needs to give the matter. If he is a shepherd to undershepherds, the word will alert him of whose flock is in danger or at risk. He can then pass on the information and pray with the pastor or overseer to determine to whom the word applies and how to aid the sheep in the situation.

Shepherd's Doctrine

No treatment of this office is sufficient without some attention given to the doctrinal responsibility of the pastor. The pastor is to feed the sheep with God's food and not man's. It is to be fresh food, free from spoilage or contaminants. The feeding is to be timely, relevant, applicable, and digestible. Several means of dispensing the Lord's manna to His people should be adopted.

Bible Studies, prayer groups, mid-week meetings, seminars and conferences, audio and video teachings, and print media are all reliable, innovative means of nurturing the flock of God. The pastor, like the nursing mother or food preparer of the house, is to test the word. In the way a natural parent smells and tastes some portion of the food before it is served or prepared to ascertain its freshness and safety, the pastor is to do the same. He is not to embrace a teaching simply because it is popular, profitable, or palatable. It is to be accepted on the basis of its wholesomeness and quality nourishment of his family. When proving a doctrine, a pastor should keep the following things in mind:

1. The nature, geographical mix, and needs of his sheep.

2. The maturity level and stage of doctrine ingestion his sheep are accustomed to and respond to readily.

3. The overall information processing methods of his sheep, such as flesh first, spirit last; the immediate now, long term later. This will tell him the manner in which the sheep will typically apply a teaching.

4. The yearning sheep have for prompt gratification, effortless learning, and quick solutions to long term problems.

5. The sheep's normal ways of translating messages and how they interpret and adopt them into their lives.

6. Sheep's aversion to Scripture intensity, extensive Bible reading, and prolonged periods in the presence of God.

7. The general lifestyle of the flock and the persuasions it tends to hold to, or to gravitate toward the fastest.

8. The trendiness or culture the doctrine happens to be linked to or flooded with.

9. Whether the doctrine has general and widespread application across the Body of Christ or if it is just effective with one group of people, or in limited geo-cultural or ethnic spheres.

10. Whether doctrine only works in restrictive situations and seems to preempt the larger part of the church.

11. Whether the doctrine overturns, mocks, ridicules, and otherwise frustrates established truth.

12.   If the word will attract to or drive the church from God's holiness, love, sanctification, service, or sacrifice.

13.   Whether or not the doctrine will sanctify or mainstream the church with the world.

14.   Whether the outcome of the doctrine will humble or inflate the flesh of the hearer.

15.   Whether the doctrine will increase the morality and modesty of the church or release its carnality in religious form.

Suggestion: Draft a present day illustration of the 15 above, and show how a novice pastor or pastoral student can discern and relate these to their present or proposed service.

Exercise:

Study various teachings that have flooded the Church over the years, and put the most influential ones through the above tests to see which ones were destined to ultimately uphold or teardown God's Kingdom truth and His Spirit.

Chapter Eight Review 1

1.   The pastor ends what? How and why?

2.   Discuss the stationary officers.

3.   What does the pastor do?

4.   What is the etymology of the word pastor?

5.   What does #4 mean?

6.   The pastor as a companion means what?

7.   Profile the true shepherd.

8.   Profile the hireling.

9. The pastorate as a format told us what about God's choice of the word?

10. Discuss the cloak, the rod, and the sling.

11. What is the essence of the shepherd's sheep management? Explain.

12. What is one key to the shepherd's success? How?

13. State the reason and the consequences of the shepherd leaving his fold.

14. Review numbers 9-12 and draft a two paragraph statement on what is to be observed in the godly shepherd.

15. Parallel and evaluate the sheep in contrast to the shepherd.

16. Discuss at length, in specific terms, the intrinsics of the pastor's being.

17. Summarize and justify the teaching on the shepherd's doctrine. Be explanative.

The Office of the Pastor

The office of the pastor, like the other four, is an ordained office. It cannot, though it frequently is, be taken upon oneself. The gifts and callings of God are without repentance. In addition to this Scripture's meaning that God does not revoke His call on a life, the passage also lets us know that these are *calls*, not enlistments into His official service. The glamour, power, prestige, and influence the pastor seems to have over his flock makes envious souls covet the office purely on the basis of these alone. Power-aspiring egoists take up the call and gather souls for selfish reasons. They wreak havoc, when they do, in the lives of those gullible enough to believe their claims of pastorship.

The officers, as we have learned from Psalm 68, are preordained. They were determined, according to this passage, even before Christ became flesh. The prophecy of His presentation of gifts to (and from among) men foretold the offices would exist. The plan of salvation, having been designed before the world began, means those elected by God to the offices were also decided on in eternity. Pre-selection called for their vessels being prepared with the faculties, gifts, talents, and abilities they would need to do the job before they entered the womb. Moreover, their pre-selection chose their destiny and the courses of life that would set them on the road to their divine call.

All of this, God did on the grounds of His predestined call and plans. While free will allows a person's option of disobeying God, and for choosing an erroneous course of life, the fixity of God's ordinations stand firm. All the spiritual accompaniments that attest to the office will not uphold or confirm the presumptuous pastorate. On the other hand, those accompaniments assigned to the person's ordained office will remain in tact and operative in them; nevertheless, being obedient to the will of the Lord. The result is of the ministers' presumption: incompatibility. The signals and influences of the ordained office will clash with presumed office and the two will negate each other. Besides that is the affect the confused minister will have on those he serves. The true fruits of the pastorate will not abound in the ministry. The incongruent mixture of the homologous dispensations causes confused, volatile influents to mold the sheep. The main reason for this has to do with the roots of the presumptuous pastor.

When the Pastorate Is Not God's

If the call is not God ordained, then it is man acclaimed. Anything coming from man himself springs from humanism, which is a definite work of the flesh. The works of the flesh, Galatians 5 tells us, are condemned by God and their practice causes one to lose his inheritance in Christ Jesus. Additionally, the root of the flesh can only bear the fruit of the flesh and those who partake of it fail to get delivered. As Christ so eloquently phrased it, "How can Satan cast out Satan?" The presumptuous officer is thus a world officer, and all that is in the world is at enmity with God because it generates no more than the things of the world in the disciple's life. (See 1 John 2) Such services may receive the applause of men and the accolades of society, but they are strictly earthbound and hell destined. Carnality and cosmopolitanism form the fabric of their service from the very beginning of the work. Keeping up with what others do, comparison, and accumulation take precedence over quality and sanctification. Numbers, possessions, and volume usurp obedience and transformation. These ministers are always looking for work and interviewing for jobs; striving toward novel trends that appeal to their followers. With no vision and lack of commitment and dedication, their need is to achieve to impress others. Prestige wins out over the word of truth and the way of righteousness.

You can always spot these institutions. They are proponents of marginalize, espousing a gray area of truth and a jaded righteousness. Worldly ministers contend the "God is love" philosophy is sufficient for salvation and preach the "no pressure, no visibility" God as their goal. You will hear from them exhortations to individuality, independence, and self reliance. For these teachers, God is just a back up to be called in times of deep distress. Worship is a convenience trip, service is as one wills, and sacrifice is tapered. Minimal disruption of the lifestyle is the order. A real lean, mean, "my own way" Christianity is what this is all about. Everything is condensed. Scriptures fit on a sliver of paper the size of a fortune cookie saying, and prayer is canned. Holiness is downplayed so as not to show off one's faith to the point of being religious. Ecumenism is its tone: all the world is saved, there is no such thing as sin, and guilt is an evil contraption of the church to keep the world from having its fun—or to intrude on it, at least. The Bible says one thing, but really means another, and Christ is not at all how the Scriptures picture Him. These ministers claim to know Him better, better than all.

Jesus is not fearsome, but loathsome. He is not holy, merely humble; not magnificent, just meek. He is not demanding, but sympathetic; not deified, only divine. He is the Lord, but safely tucked away in heaven and not at all a concern until one dies. The Father God is ancient and cannot be trusted with His own mind. Deviously, He is pictured and embraced as Old Man Time, treated as feeble and senile. His Son is still the little baby in the manger, forever glued to Mary's hip and not to be taken seriously, as He has not really grown up yet.

Do you see the confusion? It has an express purpose: to sabotage the faith of the family of God. It works because it is *confusion*. The word means "jumbled, indiscriminately mixed, poured together, to mingle." It refers to being mentally mixed up due to being unable to distinguish. Confusion is inconsistency, disarray, disorder, and distraction. It is the mix up of facts, details, events, elements, and ideas; it is indistinguishable due to lacking a sound base or discernible theme. The intent of confusion is to puzzle, confound, perplex, stymie, and bewilder. The goal of confusion, so you will know how to combat it, is to embarrass you and to shame you; to overthrow and ruin you; to defeat you and to waste you. Think about this when you try the doctrine of those things that sound so very good and feel (or make you feel) better than the day you got saved. Be wary of such doctrines because, generally, they are tingling your flesh, and this is sensual.

Sensuality, you see, is a strong feature of humanism. It feels good, it understands, and it is amenable. It is soothing and painless, easy to take and not hard on the flesh. It paints God's demands as stressful, traumatic, even catastrophic, but the world's way as unfettered and uncluttered. Contemplate these philosophies and weigh them against the word of God and you can see God's problem with them and the obvious outcome of their affect. For those standing in the office of the pastor, these views can be deadly—to themselves and to those who join themselves to such a church.

Ministers who choose the pastorate on their own are probably going to be propagating several of the above beliefs, and thereby leading susceptible (2 Thessalonians 2:2-12} souls astray. When one is called by God into his ordained office, he needs no gimmicks, no false claims, and no cunning games to play to attract and keep his sheep. All he needs is the word of the Lord, the Spirit of Truth, and a heart for the things of God.

Sheep Are Assigned, Too

In the way the pastor cannot assume his office, neither can sheep arbitrarily choose their pastors. Definitely, we are entering into hostile territory with this one. The independent stance of the modern Christian says, "I will attend the church I want and follow the beliefs that appeal to me." This is carnality. The nonsense of this contention is seen in the main definition of the word *pastor*. One of his roles is a parent. The pastor is the spiritual parent of the flock over whom he has charge. The apostles noted this position in their writings. Each one made reference to their parenthood place as the shepherd in the lives of the sheep they led.

The idea of a natural child choosing his parents is ludicrous. People for centuries have wished they could have, and many think they should be able to. Nevertheless, they cannot. Children have no say in the natural choice of their parents. Here is one of those God-made decisions settled beforehand, long before any of us were seeds in the loins of the forefathers. Inasmuch as we cannot choose our own parents naturally, nor the homes we live in, we cannot choose our spiritual parents: pastors or the churches we attend. Many sheep are sitting under the wrong shepherd. They are in the spiritual foster care system and are sorely in need of their ordained parent.

Not understanding the role of the parent in the natural will always cause the flock of God to not understand the role of the pastor. Misunderstanding will lead them to wander, to stray, to flounder, and ultimately self-pastor. The way these people treated (or treat) their natural parent is usually how they will treat their pastor. Those who have contempt for their natural parents will despise their shepherd and will likely find themselves roaming and wandering from place to place in search of that which they refuse to submit to.

Another thing is that when a natural child has balked against his parents' guardianship and nurturing because of rebellion, he will carry over that same rebellion into the kingdom of God. These offspring's resent rules, resist order, and revolt against submission. They pout at correction and fight viciously against any idea of discipline. They hate Scripture's Christian requirements and wage war against those who would hold them to the word of God. When they enter the kingdom of God, they bring their childish and brutish behaviors with them. Being older, such believers justify that same childhood abuse of authority by saying it is the result of their parent's abuse. They blame their intolerable conduct on an overbearing parent, a strict upbringing, and what they still bitterly harbor as unfair chastening. Using these childhood resentments as fuel, they rise up against anything that might bring them in order or regulate the very unruliness their parents tried to rein.

Once in the church, the pastor becomes the target. Now he gets the tantrums, pouts, and vengeance. His instructions are ignored or contested, and his authority challenged. He becomes the object of their mockery and ridicule and receives the evil treatment the natural parent received. Hebrews 12:11's revealed aim is shown to not have worked in their hearts from a child. Instead of producing the fruits of righteousness from the chastening, the person sets out on a personal vendetta against the righteousness of God. In situations like this, unforgiveness and bitterness are strongholds, especially if the parent was an unjust or a poor one.

A ragged upbringing is touted as the cause of their unruliness, in which they feel they need to protect themselves from ever being hurt in such a manner again. Whenever you see lawlessness abounding, it is the campaign of these self-righteous, unrighteous ones who sparked it and feed it with testimonies of imagined hardships and abuses divine righteousness has, supposedly, caused them. With sad embellished stories, they play on the fear of the naive and move them to join in their revolt against obedience, righteousness, godliness, and virtue. It is the rod with which they rule and abuse the pastors they take on.

For the Christian who buys into this, 2 Corinthians 6:1 becomes a sad reality: Truly they have received the grace of God in vain, for in them it failed to accomplish Titus 2:11-15. Only when there is an abiding and sincere love for the Lord will these people overcome their hostilities enough to believe God and submit to those He has chosen for them. When they do, such people are rewarded abundantly with the fruits of obedience. Their love for Christ, as Paul says, constrains them and they, like meek sheep, follow the Great Shepherd's handling of them through the undershepherd assigned to them. Then are blessings released, breakthroughs experienced, as well as peace and turnarounds enjoyed in their life. Why? Because they have demonstrated their trust in God and waited for the Lord who delivered them in the manner He so chose. In addition, they have connected in the Spirit with the pastor, whom God has not only ordained for a particular stage in their Christian walk, but in whom the Lord has deposited their spiritual gifts, blessings and provisions. In their obedience, the sheep released the flow of God from the pastor who held and nurtured them for him.

Sometimes motivated by prestige, worldly opportunity, or the insulations from sin a large congregation provides, people join a church for sheer human reasons. While the church itself may continue to reap a harvest of blessings, the misplaced sheep of the fold fail to enjoy any significant portion of it. They may be receiving some of the splash, but inwardly they know that there should be more for them, and they are not partaking of it. Most likely, it is because the shepherd they admire and chose is not the one carrying around their spiritual dispensations. He may be a friend, a family member, or a compatible charismatic leader, but he is not the one in whom the Lord pressed the wandering, wayward sheep's covenant goods. Therefore, though they may be the hardest worker, the most faithful servant, a most reliable and devoted member in the church of their choosing, they seem to be the one with the severest trials and the least rewarded for their labors.

It is true that many reasons can account for their tribulations, but an overlooked reason may be the pastor they chose. He may not be the one in whom God implanted their dispensations. It could be the vexed person was told by the Holy Spirit to go elsewhere, but because of personal bias, prejudice and advantage, they disregarded the word of the Lord, feeling that it did not matter where they attended church or in what field they served God, only that they just did.

Cases such as these call to mind what Samuel the prophet told Saul. God desires obedience over sacrifice. He condemns and harshly judges self motivated sacrifice and sees it as rebellion. Emotional saints who are guilty of this are claiming to love Jesus, but in their works, secretly, they are quiet amicable rebels whose hearts silently whisper, "Please, God, let me be *me*; don't make me change and have to go through this. Please understand my need to be me; don't ask this of me." .A wordless prayer such as this one, cried in the depths of the shallow heart, is what God is going after.

On the outside, these people praise the loudest, monopolize every conversation with how they love God, and brag about all that they do for Him. Inwardly they fear exposure and hope not to be discovered in their pretenses. They deceive many, often themselves too, because they have no idea of how strong their spirit of independence is or how powerful their need to "be me" is. So, God has to show them. He has to raise to the surface that which is buried deep within their hearts that drives them toward disobedience or self-centeredness.

Getting them to sit under the pastor He chose for them and to serve in the manner He prescribed is a good place for the Lord to start breaking their stubborn resolve. For Him to do such a seemingly simple thing like that could take years, and the person could never perform that fundamental obedience. Not doing so makes the entirety of their Christian experience a lie, and thus unprofitable in the kingdom. They, as a result, provide the Lord with creature instrumentality, but no believer usefulness.

What has all this got to do with the pastor, you ask? A great deal since, the pastor assumed by them, or assigned to them, has responsibility for dealing with these forces. Often many pastors gladly accept another's rebel sheep just to increase their own church's roll, not considering whether or not they really belong to the fold. The sincere shepherd, however, hears from and listens to God. He, on the other hand, will be told by the Lord whether to encourage a person in their resistance or to exhort them to resolve things with their old shepherd. If there is a wounding, the new pastor will accomplish the healing and then encourage the recovered sheep to return to his destined flock.

When the time comes for even one of his own sheep to leave the flock, this pastor is attuned to the Spirit of the Lord. He will, as any good parent would, begin to ready the sheep to leave the fold. At the appropriate time he will openly release the sheep in good standing and support him as much as possible in the endeavor to which the Lord called him. God's pastors will not, as so many do, take the member's leaving as a personal rejection and treat the departure as an act of treason to be condemned.

A number of other things are to be considered of the pastor, and the sheep of God's flock. Surrender to the heart, mind, and will of the Lord will attest to a pastor's genuine call and to a sheep's sincere faith and devotion to the Savior. Both constitute the basics of integrity and unfeigned love for God.

The Spiritual Parentage of Pastors

Pastors are greatly needed in the Body. Their ministry is crucial to its perpetuity and fruitfulness. The pastor receives the souls, and taking on their role as the spiritual parent, raises up the sheep in the nurture and admonition of the Lord. The pastor becomes the flock's central link to Christ, although he must be careful not to fall into the trap of displacing the Savior in their eyes. As spiritual parents, the pastor tends to, scolds, bandages, heals, leads, governs, and develops those in his care. This definition alone disqualifies many for the office. In the same way not all humans have the parenting instincts for nurturing, enriching, and overall improving the quality of a life, so too are there Christians who lack these traits. Parental cruelty, child abuse and neglect, irresponsibility, and disinterest can affect the natural and spiritual parent: The pastorate is not without its share of inadequate and incompatible servants, either.

As the spiritual parent of the new creation child of God, the pastor's influence and impact in the sheep's life will be much like that of a natural parent on his offspring. It does not matter that the pastor does not always beget his sheep; he generally inherits them. Once his own has been presented to him, the person is immediately grafted into the pastor's heart. From that moment on, a peculiar bond develops between them and is cemented by the intrinsic shepherd properties of the pastor and the innate sheep-like qualities of the sheep. They may not be social companions or business associates, but the two have a knot deeper and more inexplicable that any other. One can understand the union of marriage. One can grasp the affinity between business partners, friends, or school buddies. The basis of family ties poses no problem. The one relationship difficult to comprehend is the nature of the shepherd's influence over and love for his sheep. It is just as hard to fathom the reason for the sheep's need and devotion to his shepherd. No amount of investigation can make the matter plain. It is one of those things that has to be accepted by faith.

Whatever it is that God does between a sheep and his shepherd is for both their good. The shepherd who is without an outlet for his ministry is barren, haunted, and unhappy. The sheep without a shepherd is disjointed and vulnerable. As a natural child needs to know the love and covering of his parent, with the spiritual child it is no different. All the things a pastor is to give him over the period of time he is to sojourn in his care, the sheep is in dire need of, whether he wants to admit it or not. For the pastor it is not dissimilar. Whatever he has within him to give to those he must tend must be released. If it is not, the pastor roams through life unfulfilled and restless. Regardless of where he wishes to put his gifts and how much praise and recognition he gets for his talents, his delivery of what is within him to his flock is the only way he will know wholesomeness and peace; true enrichment and gratification.

The pastor and his sheep, when they belong together, may have a relationship not much beyond Sunday service and an occasional mid-week meeting or Bible Study. Here is the uniqueness of the arrangement the Lord puts between them. They are still strangely aware of, and drawn into, one another's existence; although their relationship, on the surface, appears to be only casual. The pastor does not have to see his sheep to feel what he feels or to know his sheep's needs. He simply spends his time with the Lord and the Lord instructs him on how to care for his sheep individually. His instincts, intuition, and sensibilities alert him to their danger or suffering. If he is a divinely appointed pastor, no matter what his flock goes through, he is an intimate part of it. The sheep too find themselves, oddly enough, in the same position. Their suffering pastor brings out all sorts of emotions in them. They fear the loss of him, dread his injury; and cannot abide by his suffering or lack. The church may be few in number or a vast congregation, but the interrelationship they share between themselves and their designated shepherd brings about a joint dependence upon one another. The pastor's family, as well, becomes important. Although they cannot explain why, his family is almost as important as their own. They care about their holidays, home, and comforts.

Until some foe of righteousness comes on the scene to tell them different, the flock is as watchful over their shepherd as he is over their souls. The wealth of spiritual advantage the Lord had told them he carries for them is more than enough motivation for the astute saint to reciprocate by tending to the pastor's material needs. Those who hold back or are fearful of serving their pastor have either had bad experiences from bad choices—for which they can blame no one but themselves—or they have little cognizance of the phenomenal role their pastor is to play in their lives before the Lord. It may take some sheep a little time, but when once they have experienced the unusual comfort, consolation, and support their shepherd carries for them, they will respond by seeing that nothing hinders or robs them of that flow.

The Lord arranged that the pastor be the vessel of the spiritual and supernatural resources for congregation's needs, and for the congregation to be the vessel of the pastor's material resources. This is a veritable mystery to those outside the church. Here is one of the many reasons why the resources in a church body are so varied and vast. They are not only to meet the needs of one another, but to see that the pastor has no material reason to abandon his post and forego his duty of feeding and leading them (See Nehemiah 13:9-14). The only reason a congregation will not uphold this part of their duty is when there is no teaching to instruct them on how the Lord wishes them to care for their gift of the pastor, or where there have been instances of pastoral abuse or neglect. While they can demand the people's sacrifices on the ground of Scripture, pastors know the fruits of demand over the beauty of desire. They realize their flock's desire to serve them is better than compulsion. The best service a pastor can enjoy is when the sheep appreciate his desire to serve the flock.

Neglected sheep are the most difficult of the two reasons to remedy. Those who need to be taught, once they have been made to understand as a body, will easily turn and begin to minister to their shepherd. With the other flock, it can be a bit harder. Neglected and abused sheep are hurt, injured, and usually bleeding. They cannot do anything for the pain they feel at their pastor's abandonment or abuse except moan. Like natural children you will find them getting into things and blaming it on the pastor, but really what they want is a reliable and trustworthy leader. Trust plays a gigantic role in the pastorate. For the sheep to come to the shepherd and open up to him, let him see and tend to their wounds, there must be the perception of safety. The pastor must have silently or otherwise guaranteed the member he is safe with him as a representative of the Lord Jesus Christ. When that trust is violated, the damage could take years to repair. Some souls never really mend, they just callous up and nurture the wound for a reminder to never again trust anyone that deeply. This is unfortunate and more harmful to the sheep than the shepherd. He will get his scolding from the Lord, repent in most cases and go on with his life. With the sheep, it is a different story. His refusal to be healed binds him in unforgiveness, hurt, and bitterness. These are like magnets to the devil, who uses them to keep the soul away from the covering and the covenant of God. The person is brutalized and battered mercilessly as the devil relentlessly recalls the incident to remind them they have no place or safety in the house of God. The agony can extend for years with a myriad of carnal remedies being tried, and one after another, failing. The only relief will come from letting go and receiving the healing and cleansing of the Lord.

The pastor on the other hand, while he has gotten his healing, runs the great risk, if he does not reform, of being abused by his church. The people may not leave, but they may not be there, either; particularly when it comes to him. Such sheep will not be able to be counted on because they feel their pastor cannot be counted on. In these instances, finance is the first place the people will punish him. Support and labor is the second. They will suddenly cut back on their sacrificial giving first. Next will be their obligatory giving. Following will be their volunteer service and free will donations. After a while, the church is struggling and the people feel it is the pastor's fault. They feel supporting the church is his problem, not theirs. Without divine intervention, the situation could go on indefinitely.

What has happened is that the people did not come to the church building, but rather to what they thought was the love and concern of the pastor. When they believed that to be dissolved, they had nothing else to identify with or relate to. So they shriveled up inside and eventually caused the congregation to do the same. When their needs ceased to be met and their pains felt, they turned inward (against the pastor) and on themselves. Unless the pastor is astute enough to correct the matter, he can pretty much say goodbye to his ministry; at least with that group of people anyway. Violated trust, broken confidences, communication breakdowns, and lack of concern are all reasons the flock will turn on its shepherd. In today's modern reinterpretation of the office, the abandonment of the flock in favor of itinerant pastoring is a big problem. However, if you notice the order of the Ephesians 4:11 offices again, you will see that the three itinerants are listed first. The pastor is fourth because the Scriptures record no itinerant pastors. He is the first introduction to the stay at home minister. By definition, the two, itinerant and pastor, are mutually exclusive. To be a *pastor* is to be stationary, to be with the people. To be an *itinerant* is to be on the road and free from the obligation of tending to and caring for a flock of believers—one definition of *pastor*. Below we will spend some time exploring the bishop's office and its many meanings.

The Pastor and The Bishop

If addressing the pastor's responsibility with doctrine was important, then covering the *pastor to pastors* is equally as important. The bishop's office has its own brand of confusion and misconception. In this section we will address some of the problems that plague its office. To include discussion of the bishop in the pastor's section is appropriate, as many pastors are, or will be, bishops. That being the case, the executive pastoral functions attached to multi- church leadership need to be addressed in God's organization and structure of His modern church.

The first problem with the typical view of the bishopric is the automatic conclusion that a bishop doubles as an apostle. Here is where we will begin our discussions.

Confusion over just who and what the apostle is has led people to take a bishop as one. To understand the role of the bishop, however, over the mission mandate of the apostle is to show two different employments of the officers entirely. The apostle is a founder, a builder, and a restorer of the lost or stolen dominions of God. He must initiate and instigate, and be the originator or restorer of his movement. His is a mandate to overthrow. The key impact of the Apostolic Move is **displacement and overthrow**. They restore the flock to God and restore kingdoms to His reign. This definition is fundamental to an apostle's move. As such, the apostle has enormous spiritual backing from God and his heavenly hosts. His ministry is upheld with supernatural powers which he uses to uphold the churches he founds and covers. The ministry is not merely deliverance, healing, and miracles, but restorative, redemptive and replete with declarative powers, also.

The apostle's fruit attests to his full embodiment of the church movement to be born out of his makeup. He integrates, for his mission, the whole realm of the church's dispensation to accomplish God's reasons for dispatching him. Besides, the apostle's headship is akin to that of Jesus Christ, in the same way Moses was to Jehovah. In the earth, the apostle is Moses sent away from home with a mission, a message, and a mandate.

A study of Moses' achievements beyond the ten plagues is baffling to the rigid thinker's natural mind. The man single-handedly set up government, established law, interpreted divine will, enforced obedience, interacted with the supernatural, attended to the needs of God, and erected the most powerful institution on earth: the nation of Israel, God's own nation. He taught, trained, drilled, and skilled a vast citizenry to break through the ranks of antiquity and shake and take kingdoms for God. Thus the apostle is the intimate companion of the Most High in the affairs of earth and man. He guides, directs, envisions, and invades. He dispenses power, delegates authority, and appoints and assigns leaders. To very few of these things can the bishop lay claim.

Here are some other drastic differences between the two. The bishop frequently has not founded his work. If he has done so repeatedly, he most likely is an apostle, and not a bishop. Bishops are often assigned and rise up from the ranks of pastor, a stationary office in the five-fold. Consequently, world vision, a primary focus of the apostle's office, is generally not the view of the bishop. His view is his district, his region, and his denomination. If the bishop is destined to ignite a new move, it will not be with the missionary spirit of the apostle, but reformative or the revival of the status quo. New moves are invariably apostolic, and don't perpetuate the old. They remove its prominence and influence in the church of God. A pastor embarking on a mission of church planting is an agent of expansion, not a minister of restorative change; and to the apostle, change is always the edict.

Bishops ordinarily do not establish the orders and governments they administrate. Usually they have a portion of a greater work they are assigned. If the bishop (misnomer in this instance) founded his works and there are many works he is credited with starting, he will have bishops he assigns to different areas and regions, as well as pastors. While this is another aspect of the apostle's office, the founding of a work or even a series of works on their own do not make an apostolic ministry. Bishops may found a number of churches that extend a present move or merely give them the empire they desire out of God's kingdom. This is not the only thing an apostolic move entails. The mix must be change, displacement, overthrow, and restoration. The drive must be a dominion driven mandate from the Lord to take back what was taken from God and to seal it that it may remain under His domain and accessible to his rule. It is highly unlikely that this would be a bishop's mandate. Founding alone is not the primary aim of the bishopric, but government, oversight and perpetuity are. Their charge is ecclesiastical order, effective government, church management, believer social order, successful public life, and maintenance of that which the apostle has started. In many cases the bishop has nothing to do with the establishment of the institutions he oversees; he is just keeping things going. He a not even apt to initiate new governments or institute new policy. The polity of most organizations has been established for years;

meaning, the bishop's role in legislation is limited. Much politicking on his part will be needed for him to enact any appreciable change in an established organization.

A bishop's powers and influence, however, should not be underestimated. His maintenance and preservation responsibilities are huge. They can make administrative and some executive, as well as operational, decisions and changes that have tremendous impact. Shifting pastors, reordering local church hierarchy, and appointing and displacing subordinate leadership can send shock waves through an organization. Their authority can totally disrupt their regions. Jurisdictional authority alone can uproot families and change the entire geographical complexion of their organization. Prayerfully, they will wield such power and authority wisely, discriminately, and to the glory of God.

The bishop's disciplinary powers also must not be slighted. Using whatever systems in place at his disposal, he can disemploy, affect income, modify expenditure, and even downscale a church's economy. He can demand attendance, divide apportionments on the basis of his own merit system, and sway his organization's overall transactions and balance of power. Finally, the ecclesiastical duties of the bishop see to divine requirements, church order, morality and ethics, and set the tone for the community life of the church. He may or may not have prescribed the precepts he governs with, yet his moves are no less effective.

Apostles innately incorporate the bishopric, according to Acts chapter 1 and 1 Peter 5. However, the assumption the reverse is true is not so. Apostles are universal, essentially. Most bishops are district or regional in their jurisdictional authority. Occasionally they are national, but rarely. The apostle is commissioned by God; the bishop, usually by his church. The broadest possible power a bishop exercises is derived from his council position and is the collective disbursal of the entire group. Autonomously, the bishop's powers are narrow in scope and are exclusively confined to his district's assignment of the church he belongs to.

In conclusion, the features and operations of the prophet are not mentioned in the list of bishopric activity, although he may have the gift of prophecy working in him. However, to remain consistent with the overall definition of the apostle, obvious attributes of the prophet's mantle must be seen in bishops to further substantiate their claim to apostleship.

Elders, Council, and Presbytery

To finalize the discussion of the pastorate, inclusion of the *elders* (a common term used interchangeably to identify the pastor) is appropriate. To begin, the elder is an active manager of public affairs. In the church under the New Testament, he is called a *presbytery*, the Greek counterpart of the word. In the Old Testament, under the regimes of natural Israel, the elders included politicians, police, government officials, religious leaders, scholars, and teachers. Even the prophet, broadly speaking, was considered part of the eldership of the people. Anyone who was older with wisdom for leadership, insight for government and management, and learned was viewed as an elder.

In the New Testament church, the term and its functions are considerably narrowed. Elders were ministers who served more in an administrative/executive capacity. Government and operations were their main concern. If the individual elder was distinguished from the council, his independent actions would be modified by his obligation to the group. In the church, the elders were ministers distinguished from deacons and not necessarily classified as pastors. They could incorporate the bishopric, the deaconry, the pastorate, and apostleship. Representation could extend to the prophets and teachers. Anyone with an aptitude for the responsibilities of headship of the organization could be considered for church eldership. Widely speaking, anyone who was in leadership, in the remotest capacity, could be seen as part of its eldership.

It is in this far-reaching context that the church today generally applies the term elder. Often its use, in this sense, is inappropriate as many ministers invoke the title implying they are part of a large presbytery, and thus sit in council over the affairs of a church. A pastor, for instance, could be an elder, but being an elder did not in early days automatically make one a pastor.

The term properly applies to the General Council of Church Leaders. Elders and council, research shows, seem to go hand in hand. However, the term disregards, as stressed earlier, the pastorate, a church itself, or its ministrations in the strictest sense. It appears to be functional in matters of the church's government, management, discipline, and preservation. Stability, prosperity and perpetuity, structure, and order are the objects of the council of the church once it has been established.

In modern society elders or councils, as classically used, would be compared to the directors or trustees of a corporation. The titles and non council work of the board members are irrelevant in respect to their collaborative aim to unify and uniform the organization they represent.

Directors, doctors, lawyers, business people, and politicians may comprise a secular board of trustees or directors. Yet, when they convene for business, none of their titles or positions take pre-eminence over the proceedings of the sessions; ideally, it should not. The typical board's chairman could be a salesperson by profession, while the one who is chairperson of a company may be a committee person. The functionality of the group and the good of the whole prevail and take precedence over personal merit and achievement in an effective board. Ability, knowledge, experience, and expediency are the primary goals of its members, both individually and collectively.

In like manner is the eldership of the church to be viewed. Whether one is normally a bishop, a deacon, or a pastor is not as important as whether he or she is qualified and competent for the position. If he or she can serve well as a useful member of the group is the first criterion. A member's congregational office should have only limited bearing on the composition and emphases of the council, while as a rule, it should include other professionals also for well-rounded representation and expertise. Nevertheless, what each one does occupationally should not dramatically impact the proceedings of the board.

For council service, each member ordinarily was seen to vacate, for a time, his normal position to unite for the collective discharge of the business of the organization he belonged to. Once their purpose was completed, the council dispersed, though not disbanded, to resume their customary work.. If a member was a pastor, then he would return to his congregation to resume his pastoral duties, which may or may not be affected by his eldership. If he was a deacon, the same thing was true. The meeting the member may have conducted with the elders gave no importance to his regular duties whatsoever.

The bishop had the same situation. His service tenure with the elders could conceivably not have much to do with his bishopric unless he was also an officer on the council and that function included his stead as bishop. For example, that a member is over a district of 23 churches may not mean anything when he enters closed sessions with the council of elders.

Wisely the council is maintained by a core of stationary members of the Body. It may not be officially governed by itinerants whose field obligations may hinder their attendance responsibility. Itinerants may be unable to report on short notice to emergency meetings or be unavailable for crises sessions. The local or nearest members, for this reason, may be the ones to carry on emergency governments and expedite the pressing affairs of the ministry.

The New Testament Elder

The New Testament uses the terms *elders* and *presbytery* interchangeably. Eventually the church settled on the predominate use of the word *presbytery*, which is the Greek form of *elder*. No doubt, an effort to divest itself of its Judaic roots and holds moved the church to exclusively use this word over elder. The early church, to establish its identity, sought to set itself apart in the minds of the people, and thus distinguish the New Covenant Church from the persuasions of Judaism in many ways. Opting to focus on one thing over another was a common method used to downplay Judaism and emphasize Christ.

When the Jews used elder, they meant it to include the entire spectrum of Jewish society. For the church it is somewhat different. The church's impact can only be overtly felt through the realm of the spirit. Natural holds remain for the time being, the domain of the sons of darkness primarily. To impact them, the church must enter through the door of the spirit. That is to say, before she can affect the earthly in a natural way, prayer must successfully precede politics and revolt. Fasting must loose the devil's holds and give power to the church's vote. Faith must relegate intellect and culture, and the spirit must overtake, first, the flesh. This strategy must be implemented and kept up if the sons of light hope to challenge, confront, and defeat the kingdoms of the world. These factors mean the influence of church presbytery is limited, confined mainly to the supernatural and the spiritual where the real battle takes place.

Composition and Rule of the Elders Council

All bishops do not have automatic seats on the typical presbytery council. Those whose capacities have nothing to contribute may not be part of the group. All five-folders may not be affected by the existence of the presbytery, although the apostle and the pastor, more than the others, will find it difficult to avoid encounters with the elders of a church. The apostle will experience this even more than the pastor.

The reason is that apostles, as founders of their works or possessors of their restorative authority, will appoint pastors and bishops in the ministry they establish or oversee. As a result, the apostle will be integral to the presbytery himself. Pastors, on the whole, may not be, as the flood of independent pastors in society mean they are disorganized and largely accountable to no one but themselves. Those pastors who are part of an apostolic move will not have such liberty or responsibility. They enjoy all the benefits and securities that accompany the insulation of the "law of large numbers." Shared resources, solid networking, collective prayer and spiritual insight, and the refinements that come from organization are some of the advantages of a council and the associations it brings about.

Independents can suffer severely, in comparison to the organization pastor, at the hands of others as lone ministers. Isolation and alienation can be two tactics Satan uses to overthrow them and their work. The years it takes to single-handedly build a lone organization into a thriving institution can take their toll. Many give up in defeat. Financial woes, resource voids, and non support drive most of these ministries out of business. Only those with a definite call, a specific mandate, and a distinct purpose in God's destiny book can overcome such horrendous obstacles and survive, or excel, as an independent. Even these ministries will have to confess they did so through an informal network of helpers, friends, counselors and support, which still constitutes an unofficial or informal board.

Research will show that a leadership presbytery is part of divine order, while countless people who have suffered their abuses vehemently object to them. The truth is, no ministry can be successful without them. The book of Revelation reveals the Heavenly Board of Elders: the Celestial Sanhedrin, as it is called. It identifies them as the 24 elders of creation. Daniel's prophetic book alludes to a similar celestial presbytery comprised of watchers who judged and chastened Nebuchadnezzar for his pride.

Israel's new kingdom, by the same token, was scarcely out of Egypt before Jehovah disclosed its hierarchal order to Moses who received confirmation of the plan from Jethro, his father-in-law. The leadership void was to be filled, finally, with the institution of the 70 elders. The order was Moses, Aaron, and Miriam; Joshua, Caleb, and Hur; Aaron's two sons, Abihu and Nadab; and the 70 elders (See Exodus 24). Miriam's inclusion in the top leadership of Israel is seen in Micah 6:4 and implied in Numbers 12:1-3. These made up the nation's initial ecclesiastical, political, and social leadership.

Over time, theocracy gave way to monarchy, but the elders remained intact throughout the centuries as central to Israel's leadership order. This was true right up to, and including, the Sanhedrin on earth. Captivity caused the political and spiritual to divide, so the nation's monarchy was no longer supplied from their own brethren. Now foreigners were their secular leaders. The effect of this was to downgrade their governmental and political influence and leave the sphere of their headship mostly in the realm of the spiritual. A divorce, as Pilate's trial with Christ shows, had taken place between the ecclesiastical/spiritual and the secular, and the people of God were the losers because of it.

Nevertheless, eldership is intrinsic to any order God establishes, and it will continue until Christ's kingdom is set up on earth. He promised the apostles, for example, that they would be the eternal elders of the nation of Israel upon her redemption. He said they would sit on the twelve thrones of Israel when He came into His kingdom. Revelation prophecies show kings and elders will govern the new world as God and Christ remain in the background, like Moses, for the more difficult matters. A heavenly priesthood will continue to praise, thank, and serve God for His eternal victory. The Church as Christ's Bride will tend to her groom forever. The Holy Spirit will dispense God's life, truth, and love for all ages as the eternally dispatched member of the Godhead. There will be kingdoms, countries, nations and kings. Spiritual power will again meld with flesh to bring to pass the Father's intent from the start. Order will reign, organized power will rule, and glorified humans will do it. The same 24 elders who governed God's handiwork from the beginning will remain, with their human counterparts reigning beneath them.

Yes, elders are basic to any of God's leadership and should be respected and embraced by Christ's church. Even the world understands the detriment of disorganized power in authority, operations, and government. Anarchy and revolt are regular members of such a society. The church suffers from these two foes of leadership constantly. Modern individuality—libertinism—has led to many disruptions and church takeovers in the Body of Christ. A good amount of this destruction can be blamed on disorganized power.

The church is the most powerful entity on earth. There is, without question, no greater institution in existence than the church of Jesus Christ. With all heaven backing her and filling her, there just is no way to annihilate the church apart from the murder of the Godhead. That was tried once and didn't work. The only successful means of attack against the church comes through separation. Divide and conquer, the devil knows, is still the best way to infiltrate and take the reins of the kingdom of God away from her. This Satan does through the lady's arch enemy, herself, through the flesh.

KEY CLOSING QUESTIONS

1. When is a pastor a bishop?

2. When is a bishop an apostle?

3. Cite the differences between the two, in reference to #2 above.

4. Draft a feature profile of the pastor, bishop, and apostle.

5. Discuss the elder/presbytery lecture.

6. Order a ten-year-old ministry that has just taken on three additional churches, two schools, and five other enterprises. There is an original board of three people and the new organizations all have their respective leaders who must be retained.

Chapter Eight Review 2

1.   State the errors of taking the pastorate upon oneself.

2.   Outline some key features of the pastorate that is not God's.

3.   Describe the Lord's problems with the perceptions of #2.

4.   Overview the discussion on confusion.

5.   Explain the traits of sensuality and its conflict with spirituality.

6.   Summarize the discussion on Sheep assignment in depth.

7.   Give the significance of the spiritual parentage of pastors.

8.   Describe the nature of the fundamental relationship between the pastor and his sheep.

9.   What is the resemblance between the pastor and the bishop?

10.   State how the bishop is, or is not, an apostle.

11.   Narrate the distinctions between the foundations and officiations of the two (the apostle and the bishop).

12.   What is an elder?

13.   What is an elder *not*?

14.   Give the reason elders are a necessary part of the Church.

15.   Why are apostles and elders the main ones likely to interact with an eldership?

16.   How is the law of large numbers helpful to eldership organization?

17.   Review the problems independents suffer.

18.   Discuss the eternal origins of eldership.

Pastoral Analyses

l. Pastors may or may not be the founders of the churches they pastor. For them this is not a prerequisite, or a requisite for that matter. They are chosen to tend the sheep and will see their congregation turnover repeatedly throughout their years of service.

2. Pastors can pastor several churches at one time. In this instance they are bishops and have undershepherds installed in each one of their churches. Just because one is a bishop does not mean he is an apostle. Refer to earlier discussions to understand the basis for this statement.

3. Pastoring emphasizes the post conversion care of the sheep. Many pastors have not begotten their sheep but have inherited them through a variety of means. Nevertheless, they are the ones who concentrate on discipling the sheep for Christ, by that the new creation life they are given will be developed and enriched for eternal life and everlasting productivity.

4. Generally, pastors are deeply involved in the lives of their congregants, something many of them would like to avoid but can't. The nature of the sheep and the order of their office demands they be in intimate contact with those they shepherd for God. To be diligent, attentive, and effective, the pastor must see that as little distance and as brief a separation between himself and his sheep occurs as possible.

5. The maturity, stability, and the fundamental enrichment of the sheep is the aim of the pastor's office. He is their guide, their leader, their example, and their teacher. Bringing them into the fullness of the Godhead is the ultimate aim of the endeavors and programs the pastor employs to serve his Body of believers.

6. Pastors are firm, sometimes stern; however, their over-involvement in the lives of those they pasture, and their intimate knowledge of the events and details of their life, can make some pastors preferential and bias in their treatment of the sheep. Also, because of these reasons, the pastor is prone to shield what he believes to be his feeble or extraordinary sheep from everything and everyone, even God. This danger is what God anticipated when he ordained that all the five-fold officers participate in ministering to His church so that His flock would not be stunted by short-sighted and temperamental leadership. For this reason the pastor regularly needs to have the ministry of the prophet, and the others, in his church.

7. Order, authority, government, organization, and leadership characterize this office. Regardless of how souls resent it, the pastor's mandate includes ruling in tenderness and with patience over the sheep. The reason is not because the pastor is better at bossing or controlling people, but because of what we have learned in this book about sheep. They stray, they wander, they are inflated by their worldly achievements, and they are embittered by their sufferings. All these things the pastor needs to temper and relieve the sheep of during his leadership of them. A basic contempt for authority, joined by an underlying contempt for God and the things that pertain to Him by carnal souls, make most believers difficult to nurture and correct. James 4 says that the world is at enmity with God, while Paul revealed in the book of Romans that the natural mind is at enmity with God. The two together make for a potentially explosive and hostile environment which the pastor must tame. Furthermore, the apostle Paul told us in 2

Corinthians that the natural man does not receive the things of the Spirit of God and finds them foolish. It is because of the aggregate of all these, mostly unknown to the flock, that the pastor must possess authority to enforce obedience to the word of the Lord in his church and to bring the sheep up in the nurture and admonition of the Lord. Moreover, the safety and well being of the flock make it essential to establish order and government to regulate unruly and damaging behavior and avoid contamination of the flock by insidious forces that creep in from time to time.

8. Nurturing, development, liberty, holiness, and discipleship service are paramount to the Pastoral Anointing.

9. The teaching anointing, if cultivated, is to be present within this office. Pastors can hardly complete their charge if they are not apt to teach, which the Scriptures tell us all servants of God are to be. Teaching the sheep the elementary principles of Christ, the fundamentals of the kingdom of God, the patterns of godliness, Christian conduct and morality, and church doctrine and sacraments are the constants every pastor's curriculum should have. The fruit the sheep as a whole bear alone testifies to the effectiveness of the pastor's ministry. 2 Corinthians 3 says it well: The best commendation a pastor can hope to receive is the written epistle of his labors on the hearts of those he touches as seen through their lifestyles.

10. Of necessity, pastors are people oriented and congregation minded. Pastors live with their people more than any other office, and bear the burden of carrying incessantly their burdensome lifestyles. They are paternal (and maternal) in nature and are usually protective of the flock in their leadership. Pastors strongly influence the behavior and beliefs as well as the devotion of those in their charge. Because of this pastors generate intense love or resentment from those they minister to.

Exercise:

Using the information from this section, draft a two-day conference for a graduating class of pastors. The goal is to orient them to their office and strengthen their new identity.

Chapter Eight Review 3

1.	Numbers 1-3 of the Pastoral Analyses tell you what critical things about the pastor?

2.	Why are pastors deeply involved with their congregants?

3.	How and why can pastors sometimes be over-shielding of their sheep?

4.	What five things characterize the office and why? Relate your answer to the carnal man.

5.	Explain the necessity of the pastor being people minded.

Personality of the Office

1. Pastors are adept at people interaction and stress godly development.

2. Pastors who know the gravity of the office and the weight of their charge commit themselves to acquiring extensive biblical knowledge and spiritual insight. They know they will need both to feed the flock of God with His knowledge and understanding and to present their sacrificial offerings of redeemers holy and sanctified and acceptable to the Lord, thereby bringing to the throne vessels God can relate to and interact with Himself.

3. A devoted pastor has a heart for understanding what God desires for His people and an ear to hear it. His mind is willing to provide for, and produce in them, what God desires. Good pastors know and remember that they are really undershepherds, for the flock belongs to the Lord. They therefore will not treat the flock harshly, nor intrude on their union with God. The pastor will make every effort to see that the Lord can enjoy His purchased possession and that the sheep do not fall into the habit of deliberately and indifferently offending the Spirit of the Lord. The wise pastor knows for them to do so is to incur God's chastening on the sheep, and on himself. Both can make him responsible for broken fellowship between the sheep and God.

4. The pastorate requires extensive leadership and guidance, which calls for critical thinking, situation analysis, evaluation and problem solving skills. Pastors resolve disputes, identify sin, remedy shortfalls and downfalls, and make judgment on the routine executions of the Christian life. They are conscious of the seriousness of error and realize that no matter what they feel, think, or believe, it is the Lord who must attest to the truth of His word and the quality of their leadership.

5. Pastors, as protectors of the flock, are the spiritual guardians of the Lord's sheep. They must remain genuine defenders of the veracity of the faith. Pastors must ever be on guard against heresy, apostasy, reprobation, and congregant lethargy. They must be insightful enough to spot carnality and bold enough to confront and condemn it. The pastor needs to shoulder the weak sheep and shore up their faith and devotion along the way. He must balance the Body's apportionments so that the strong do not gobble up the provisions and privileges of the weak, and see that there is equity in all distributions to avoid fostering a feeling of unfairness, favoritism, and elitism within the fold.

6. The teaching and preaching demands of the office means pastors are excellent communicators and teachers. The anointing they have for the office makes pastors acutely aware of how God wants to develop His flock. Their familiarity with the flock enables them to perceive their needs, understand their deprivations, and strive diligently to resolve both. The pastor is inclined to beneficial counseling, and when learned, is able to deftly impart the wisdom of God to those in his charge. His compassionate nature makes him interested in their concerns and his attentiveness makes him a good listener to their problems. Study and practice will help the pastor produce eloquent delivery styles and effective transmission of the doctrines of God.

7. Pastors must subscribe to impeccable morality, ethics, and integrity. The supreme obligation of any minister is to show the difference between Christ and the world,

between righteousness and sin. The pastor must be an example of the living Christ in word and deed, and have God's standards of morality and godliness. A sagacious pastor will customarily purview the long term affects of a practice or action and be able to say with certainty what is or is not of God, and therefore allowable in his church. He should, if he is a servant of God, maintain a righteous atmosphere in which his flock may grow, be secure, and be well preserved. The pastor's assent, consent, or dissent is all it takes to swing a church from holiness to worldliness. He must, because of this, endeavor to cultivate high discernment to know the difference between good and evil and make the distinctions clear for those he shepherds. In line with this, the pastor must also be honest, dependable, impartial, and godly in his dealings. He must not give the sheep the impression that there is one standard for himself and another for them. Furthermore, he must not involve himself in shady dealings and by example teach the flock of God to sin. Moreover, the pastor should avoid silently or doctrinally teaching the flock to rebel against the Lord, or give them ungodly license to pervert the laws of God, the way of righteousness, and the truth of God's word ever open for them.

8. Pastors must always keep to God's standard of holiness and consecration. The sheep will look to their shepherd for propriety, virtue, rectitude, and integrity. They will expect the pastor to teach it and keep it. The inward unction of the Holy Spirit within will tell them the right and wrong way. The pastor himself must, therefore, be submitted to the leadership and government of the Holy Spirit so as not to conflict with His inner teachings in the sheep. To cause a conflict between God and His sheep by deviating, compromising, or watering down the truth of God's Word is to stand in the way of the sheep's salvation and block the way of righteousness. No minister has the liberty to overturn what God has decreed, instructed, or defined for His sheep, when once that message has been found in the Bible. In addition, the pastor is not authorized to lift divine restrictions or to rival the truth of God with double-sided teachings. He must take care not to allow in the churches what God has condemned in the Word. He must not give permission for what God has said He will judge and not endorse what the Holy Spirit will chasten, as these things will bring on undue suffering and hardship in the lives of the sheep from God, who has said He will recompense all sin, even error.

9.   Pastors are people of great fortitude, rectitude, perseverance, and character. They, by nature, must be disciplined, dedicated, and full of restraint and self-control. The high activity demands of the office show the pastor's stamina and energy are uncharacteristically high. They are able to press and keep going when most of their flock has collapsed. On account of this, the pastor can easily overtax his reserves and suffer fatigue-related illness. Wisdom dictates that he order his life, schedule his workload, distribute and delegate as much as possible, and know when he has reached his limit. The pastor's ability to discharge his office depends upon his physical well being, sound emotional state, and positive psychological outlook. These are greatly affected by stressful situations, poor body maintenance, and an unrelenting ministry pace. In addition to wearing the resistance of the pastor down, he will find his patience growing thin, his prayer life diminishing, and his study being eliminated by the pressures of his service. The sheep can easily became the object of his imbalance, and the church's welfare will suffer as a result.

10. Pastors are to be loyal, humble, and meek. They are to possess conviction and resiliency, especially in view of the up and downs close relations with people can cause. The fluidity of human emotion and the mutable nature of the church means the work of the pastor is never static. He must become accustomed to change, to opposition, to resistance, and to the unexpected. Broken friendships and relationships, unanticipated

events, and the like threaten the constancy of the ministry always. Sheep uprising and resentment can shrink his membership overnight, and his finances along with it. All these things are unsettling and the pastor has to know when he starts out who he serves and why he is doing what he is doing. In the face of harsh climatic conditions, the pastor must stand firm on his resolve and not waver or succumb to the temptations of the devil to veer him off his determined and predestined course.

Nature of the Office

1. Overseer, governor, leader
2. Administrative executive.
3. Disciplinary, developmental corrections
4. Consultative and instructional
5. Resource training ministry preparation
6. Church rites and sacraments
7. Appointments and installation
8. Membership communal life, family development, kingdom sociability
9. Community involvement to reach the neighborhoods they settle
10. Interaction and interfacing with the people to encourage church attendance
11. Outreach
12. Missions, relief services, crisis intervention
13. Educational programs, member enrichment
14. Christian maturity and stability
15. Facilities oversight and preservation
16. Member support

Exercise 1:
Design a ten-point Pastor's Training Program to last three weeks using the personality of the office.

Exercise 2:
Draft a pastor's ministry that integrates, applies, and exhibits the 16 points stated under Nature of the Office.

FINAL PROJECT

The Pastor's Office

A.   Students: First take the survey yourself in class, and discuss it afterward as a group, comparing the answers among yourselves and with the book.

B.   Next, administer the survey to five pastors of your choice.

C.   Then compile the data from your survey and write a report on those you surveyed, contrasting it with what you learned in class. The report should include comparisons, observations, the state of the contemporary officer, his needs, strengths, weaknesses, and concentrations. The report should conclude with a general student analysis and an overall recommendation for the improvement and enrichment of the modern pastor.

Report is to be typed, at least three pages, have a cover sheet, have reference and comparative analyses, charts, and profiles.

Pastor's Interview Questionnaire

Date_____

Name_____

Address_____

Denomination_____

Years in Service_____   Size of Ministry_____   (S M L)

INTERVIEWER SURVEY

1. How did you come to be a pastor?

2. What 3 things do you believe a God ordained pastor should know, practice, and preach?

3. What do you feel is a shepherd's major responsibility?

4. What do you feel are the five most critical responsibilities of a sheep?

5. The phrase, "pastors are spiritual parents" means what to you?

6.   What is the difference between a pastor and a bishop?

7.   What is the difference between a pastor and an apostle?

8.   What is the difference between a pastor and an elder?

9.   Give 7 main features to be found in every person who is a pastor.

1._____   2._____   3._____

4._____ 5._____ 6._____7._____

10.   What 10 things would you say are part of every pastor's personality?

l._____   2._____   3._____

4._____   5._____   6._____

7._____ 8._____ 9._____

10._____

11.   Outline 5 elements that define the nature of the pastor's office.

1._____   2._____   3._____

4._____ 5._____

*Thank you for helping me complete this assignment!

Chapter Eight Review 4

1. Explain item #2 (under the personality of the office)in illustrative terms.

2. What causes God's chastening on the pastor and his flock?

3. Give the reason for the leadership skills the pastor needs.

4. The pastor as the spiritual guardian of the Lord's flock involves what?

5. Explain the need for pastors to be excellent communicators and teachers.

6. List several things affected by pastoral morality and integrity.

7. What drawbacks exist in the pastor relaxing his standards?

8. Name the things that can negatively affect the Church's welfare and the pastor's role in it.

9. What can, and is intended to, veer the pastor off course? How are the sheep and circumstances responsible for it?

CHAPTER NINE
The Teacher

The Teacher

Introduction

The teacher's office is the last of the five-fold officer's ministries to be addressed. It is the staple of the church. For only through teaching can the Body grow, function, and progress. Matthew 28:20, the second half of the Great Commission, tells Christ's disciples to "teach the nations." But what are we to be teaching? We are to teach Christ's commands, and why and how believers are to observe the law of obedience; to heed the voice of the Spirit; and to obey the commands of the Lord.

The mark of recognition for the true teacher of the Lord is his intuitive apprehension of the importance of God's desire for the knowledge that produces holiness, righteousness, sanctification, and service. The next thing he will be concerned with getting across to the church is who Christ is and why He came, who the Father is, and the believer's relationship to Him. Following these are other areas of importance that center on teaching students what to do as new creation children of God. Helping them learn how the new creation kingdom is to be nurtured, established, and developed in the spiritual and earthly practices of the God-centered life in Christ is next. Lastly he will be concerned with assuring the believer's knowledge and perspectives on the end time and the afterlife are correct. Also, the teacher would want Christ's saint to understand what risks his inheritance in Christ Jesus.

Kingdom living is uppermost in the mind of the teacher. His focus is on the wisdom, knowledge, culture, and perspectives of the divine in relation to the Godhead's inhabitation of the Body of Christ on earth. The teacher desires its reverent, enlightened response to God's unctions, will, purposes, plans, and needs. They know that knowledge is what will aid this. What eternity is all about, the truth versus the lie, and the way the believer is to handle Satan, the flesh, and the world to successfully conduct his or her new creation life are final thoughts the teacher has of how to educate and cultivate the Body of Christ. These, he knows, increase the church's enjoyment of their inheritance.

Essentially, these sum up the subjects teachers in Christ are to be concerned with above all else. Needless to say, if the people cannot read or function effectively in their society, the teacher is charged with removing their darkness (ignorance) and equipping them to survive, contribute to, and participate in their culture. For the Redeemed of the Lord, this means in the kingdom of *life* and not death; in the kingdom of *Christ* and not Satan's. Basic skills, also, are not to be neglected or ignored by the Christian teacher, yet these are all to be taught against the backdrop of Christ's kingdom, God's truth and righteousness, and His holiness (See Daniel chapter 12). It helps us apprehend the Lord's design for His teachers.

The Office of the Teacher and Christian Education

The field of Christian education has boomed over the last decade or so. Much material, training, lecturing, and attention has been devoted to the subject. It is as if the church has discovered anew the importance of teaching and education to the fruitful Christian life. Much of the information has been useful and helpful; however, not all of it has been wholesome or expedient for the Body of Christ. A large part of the teaching realm presently dominating the church has a destructive secular bent that has the effect of taking the believer's eyes off the Lord and centering them on himself, the world, and on the flesh.

The advent of the sciences has had much to do with this outcome. That is not to say that the sciences in and of themselves are inherently sinful. Actually, the opposite is true. Scientists have the imperative function of teaching the Lord's creation about Him. They are charged with exploring and leading society in discovering valid, basic facts about its origins and existence. The whole aim of the field, as the Lord intended, was to allow man to point humanity's gropings and search of its last identity and knowledge to its Creator. The idea of science or any other branch exalting itself above the knowledge of God and standing in the way of a person's discovery of, and reunion with, his Creator is the result of the unbelief Satan deposited in man. Human self-obsession and the quest for self-deification is the product of the laws of sin and death at work in him (See Ezekiel 14). This was positively *not* the Lord's goal of education.

The Lord's aim for education then is to "lighten the darkness born in every soul, and thus preserve and protect the society it belongs to." The emphasis of this goal is to be on the revelation of God, the establishment of morality, the institution of law and order, and the functionality and sociability of its citizenry. These are all to be accomplished through the revelation of knowledge, which is thus the discovery of God. Education's aim is **knowledge, wisdom, insight, understanding, application, and utility.** Its chief activities are teaching and instruction, training, and example. Education brings about study, research, exploration, contemplation, and deliberation. Students encouraged to practice involve themselves in the compilation and application of knowledge.

When we speak of Christian education, we bring into the above range of activities the subjects of **God, creation, salvation, sin, righteousness, redemption, sanctification, morality, and truth over facts.** The Christian educator must add to his curriculum of teaching the introduction of the creature to its God. It is the Christian teacher who knows enough to reverse the darkness of sin and death in a life through the intellect and educate the student in the proper priorities of divine life.

The Void Left by World Teachers

The teacher's charge for these reasons is great. The Bible says they will have the harsher judgment far failing or neglecting to let God's unenlightened creation know about Him. The Christian teacher differs from the worldly teacher in that this accomplishment is the principal commendation he is to seek. His graduates are not stagnated, driven, discombobulated disciples of a "mishmash" of groundless information used to robotically carry out their life's work. Instead they are to be whole functioning, balanced human beings (if he has done his job well) who execute life's purpose with insight and understanding. They know who and what they are and why they were born. Their learner's experience was not an empty, dry encounter with endless facts and uncertain theories, but an interaction with the wisdom and enlightenment that brought him into being. That's to set him heart and soul, face to face, with who he is to become. This is the hallowed call of the teacher, and the mission of Christian education.

It is a blatant failure on the part of any of God's ordained institutions that His children and the lost can invest thousands of dollars and countless hours in learning sessions that leave them with more questions than answers. Graduating them with a bleak view of the future because they have not, in the course of their academia, met and understood the living God is the greatest tragedy. It seals their hopelessness. If fruit is the measurement of performance and effect, then present society has a serious indictment against its knowledge institutions—the church included. Furthermore, if society and culture vindicate the educational process, then it, too, cannot justify or acquit the institutions of learning who nurtured its populace.

The current dismal view of the future, the raucous tide of lawless irreverence, the flood of godlessness in authority; and the fame of reckless role models are all fingers pointing at the failure of instruction and training. Lost values; indifference to righteousness, order, and truth; and abuse of power, possessions, and persons all say in bright, blinking neon signs, "Somewhere, somehow, we have failed, and we don't know what to do about it." The hopelessness, helplessness, and despair all say the reign of darkness has been successful in terrorizing the world, suffocating the light, and commandeering the souls of humanity. Lastly, when ignorance, impulse, fantasy, devastating hedonism, emotionalism and such win out over prudence, restraint, discipline, wisdom, and evidential destruction, something sickening has taken hold. The promising mental capacities of humanity have been made a prisoner of sensuality.

Aside from an overall failure of the church, the institution of learning as God designed it is the culprit responsible for rampant moral decline. Several scriptures in the Bible tell us why. Let us look at a few before we move into the purpose and explanation, as well as the mission and work of the teacher. We will start with Daniel 12:2.

The Importance of Godly Teachers

Daniel was a brilliant man. He was a statesman, a scholar, a sage, and a scribe. On top of this, the man was an ardent worshiper of his God. At the end of Daniel's string of visions from the Lord, he received this word from the angel Michael: "Those who are wise shall shine like the brightness of the firmament, and those who turn many to righteousness, like the stars forever and ever." Stars are synonymous, biblically speaking, with messengers. Messengers, as used here, refer to teachers. To turn people to righteousness means *to alter their behavior and conduct*. The outside behavioral change they exhibit implies an inward attitudinal change. Changing the attitude can only be accomplished by teaching, whether by example, illustration, or lecture. What Michael prophesied to Daniel was that teaching would convert its students. Those who taught them well would make them want to convert. The teacher, he disclosed, would shine brighter than the celestial stars, and be remembered forever for his godly achievements.

So important is teaching that not only does it affect behavior, beliefs, and attitudes, it leaves the most lasting results, mainly improved or altered personhood. Cross reference the above scripture with Daniel 11:33. Jeremiah 23:22 further underscores the value and impression of teaching. He too, through God, said the effect of teaching on a learner is conversion. For more information, read over Isaiah 30:20b,21. As you can see, teaching is fundamental to God's dealings with man. From Genesis to Revelation, the subject of teaching is addressed in one way or another. God's accentuation of the matter is obviously due to Ephesians 4:18; Jeremiah 4:22; 5:1; John 1:9,10; Deuteronomy 1:39; and Hebrews 5:14. Together these reveal the bare truth about the condition of human life and the only remedy for its darkness. The only answer is teaching.

Exercise:

Study each Scripture and write an analysis of its contribution to this teaching. Include your own thoughts as well on what you discovered from the readings.

Education

Our entire educational system is based on the absence of light in mankind—light being synonymous with knowledge, wisdom, truth, and understanding, that is. Education is important to any culture. Those who are deprived of it are bound to the baseness, crudeness, vulnerability, danger, and suffering that characterize fallen natural man. Simple things are not understood by them. Things like hygiene, food preservation, protection, safety, and so on are out of their reach without education. They are precluded from healthy lifestyles, wholesome practices, and productive lives, subsisting only on the very ground God cursed way back in Genesis. Bound to the holds of darkness, they must depend upon the angry elements Adam's offense turned hostile against him. Sadly, many of these floundering souls fall prey to worshipping the elements as well, and end up abused by the vicious demons manipulating them. Education is the main solution to this state. If you were to view the state of man described above, devoid of teaching, you would easily see the areas of life the field address.

Education's Purpose

Education serves many purposes. Obviously space will not allow us to expound on all of them. However, treatment of the office of the teacher would be wanting if the officer is vague about the realm of ministry he is appointed to. A fundamental appreciation of the roots and object of education is needed if he is to approach his ministry with the right mind, and cultivate the diligence he must have to successfully perform.

From a number of sources, education is intended to provide the following enrichment and enablements to a life: knowledge, ability, training, skill, discipline, proficiency, productivity, and learning. Examining these from a deprivation and lack standpoint, you would have to realize what education addresses: ignorance, ineptitude, inability, incompetence, ill restraint, mediocrity, barrenness, and lethargy. The teacher serious about his duty has to know that his position is ordained for these reasons. He then must take steps to see that he has remedied these deficiencies in his own life before undertaking the job of removing them from the lives of others.

The effects of education are development, maturity, equipment, formation (mold & shape), conformation (fit, adjust, adapt), reformation (correct, alter, restore, improve), preparation (provide, qualify, equip, outfit, complete), and production. To teach is to accomplish all this in a life for a variety of purposes.

Education addresses one's citizenship, work, society, and culture. It enhances prosperity and ideally, productivity. Its object is the character, mind, intellect (thoughts and perspectives included), heart (emotions, beliefs, desires), consciousness, and conscience. To strip the range of teaching down to the mind only is to reflect an utter lack of insight into the natural state of man and the consequences of his ignorance. The teacher must be accepting of these fundamentals if he is to respect his office, and supply himself with the resources he needs to do his job.

When education is properly and wisely administered, it will do the following:

1. Instill the knowledge, customs, philosophies, ideals, and pursuits of the culture in the student.

2. Qualify student to partake of, to enrich or be enriched by, or contribute to their society.

3. Enable student to become a good citizen of the country and a useful member of society.

4. Cause student to desire to be able   to perpetuate and progress his society.

5. Mold student into an extended representation of the vision, purposes, mission, and concepts of the country and its society. Education accomplishes uniformity for the sake of unity.

6. Give student a knowledge of the occupations, skills, and profitabilities available in his or her world, and equip him or her to fill one or more.

7. Facilitate the student's acquisition of his or her share of the country's wealth, prosperity, prestige, and economy.

8. Establish student in his rote and station and in his responsibilities to his country to assure its continuance, advancement, solvency, and sovereignty.

9. Familiarize student with the government, history, and cultural enrichments of his culture.

10. Form student's character, mentality, attitudes, and aims to that which exemplifies the spirit of his country and/or culture.

Of course there are more, but these sum up the essence of what you need to understand. To be sure, whenever you find yourself in a learning or teaching environment, these are the least you will come away with. They are why you need to be very careful about the teachers you choose and the subjects you learn. Be sure you agree with their outcomes, their aims, and the benefits you will derive from them. Also be sure that you desire the changes, improvements, and effects the knowledge will cause in your life.

History of Education: Origin, Christian Church

In case you are wondering what this extensive information on education has to do with the office of the teacher in the Christian church, the answer is a great deal. To start, history will show that the institution of learning began with the people of God. The ancient Hebrews were the first to formalize education. They developed the primitive recitation-to-memory method of enforcing learning upon their male students. Later, church groups did the same to catechize the faith of Christ. Organized education as we know it received its foundations from the Body of Christ. Even the hallowed institutions of the world began as Christian institutions (colleges and universities). They formed originally to teach the kingdom of God, the salvation of Christ, the doctrine of life, and to equip men and women of God to go into the world and do the same. The Great Commission was their chief motivation. One world acclaimed American university cited John 17:3 as its ground of existence and fundamental aim.

None of this should come as a big surprise since the Bible tells us that the Lord is the God of knowledge (1 Samuel 2:3). Over time, the founders and their successors neglected to remain with God enough to keep expanding the knowledge they had received from Him. For the sake of expediency, they turned back to the dark knowledge they had obtained from the world. In addition, the Christians, like ancient Israel, longed to be like the nations around them, and thus wanted to learn what the world was learning. So they stopped supporting the Lord's schools and began to divert their money to the schools of the world. Sounds a lot like today, doesn't it?

The Lord's institutions of learning, because of this, had little recourse. For the sake of survival, they too joined forces with the world. They inducted secular curriculums into their programs, engaged unsaved teachers to teach them, and petitioned unsaved financiers to cover the expenses of the failing schools. Naturally, whoever held the purse strings gained control. Therefore, over time, the hallowed halls of our Ivy League institutions and other colleges, to remain open, allowed themselves to be taken over by the secular.

Although all this happened centuries ago, the history record reads like a current events article. Lack of vision caused the people to grow restless, dissatisfied, and insatiable. In their grumbling for more, they reverted back to Egypt to eat the food they had been choking and dying on for years. After awhile, in the way He responded to Israel and their temple once it had become overrun by the nations, the Lord gave His institutions (most of them) up to the enemy and gathering His glory, He departed from their place.

No one in the office of the Christian teacher should enter it unaware of this knowledge. No one starting a school for the Lord Jesus should be unaware of it, either. Moreover, anyone committing to the support of the Lord's work automatically takes on the responsibility for His approved learning institutions as well. Here is why.

We said earlier that education prepared its students for society and sought to advance the culture, stabilize the country, and equip a supply of capable and competent workers to fill its labor needs. This being the case, then, the Lord's kingdom can hardly be furnished with these if the schools that are patronized and supported are not His. The world's schools have shut God out. He has no say-so in them, as any informed citizen will tell you. The only way He is going to meet His own kingdom needs, spread His word and life, and cultivate a supply of educated, competent ministers is through His own schools. Should they be neglected, impoverished, or unattended, they too will turn themselves over to the world for support, recognition, and patronage. If they don't they will die. The death of learning is the death of the country. The teachers of the Body must know this and include it as important information to be integrated in their learning programs.

Exercise:

Draft a lecture outline to communicate the above information to a conference of skeptical Christian educators. Use it to gather support for an alliance of Christian institutions, and to solicit support economically and otherwise, for the collective success of Christian schools.

Chapter Nine Review 1

1. What makes the teacher the church's staple?

2. What is uppermost in the mind of the teacher?

3. Why is Daniel 12 helpful to the teacher?

4. Describe and comment on the section on Christian education.

5. Discuss the void left by world teachers.

6. Compare #5 with the importance of godly teachers.

7. Recount the fate of the uneducated and why they suffer this fate.

8.   Outline and illustrate the specifics of instruction.

9.   Profile the 10 point statement on what wise education will do.

10. Summarize the history of education and comment on its contribution to the state of Christianity and the world today.

The Office of the Teacher

To avoid redundancy, the substantiation for this ministry being called an office may be seen by referring back to earlier portions of this text. Also, in your reviews, refresh yourself on the meanings of *characteristic* and *personality* to recall how they apply to this officer. Look over again the explanations given for the anointing and you will understand how it relates to this position.

The Greek word for teacher, as used in our Ephesians 4:11 and I Corinthians 12:28 scriptures is *didaskalos*, which defines one who is an instructor, a teacher, a doctor. It refers to one who educates, trains, disciples, chastens and punishes a pupil, or a learner. It is also a scholar. The inference is that what makes the teacher is his enrollment of students for the purpose of teaching them. This implies a school or a school-like setting. The official aspect of the teacher surfaces in information from other words. Cross references of the word chosen for the office led to the application of a prefix, -*nomos*. In connection with the teacher, the word would be *nomosdidaskalos*, meaning an expounder or teacher on the order of, or on par with, a rabbi who ministers the law of God. Its implications infer **one who teaches by custom and thus is regarded as a professional**. The prefix -*nomos* expands the idea of teaching as meant here to include prescriptions of the law, its usage, and its regulations. In addition, it includes the principles of the Gospels and one, who through his knowledge and position, is a legislator.

Further investigation of the word uncovered the same word that amplified the office of the evangelist. It was the word *didactics*. It is a common word used in the educational circles of our society. Biblically, when the term is used, it defines the discrete elements of the teaching arena: advisory, education, and prescription. Education we have already spent time discussing. Advisory includes consultative, admonitory, exhortative, moralistic, and remonstrative teaching, as well as the cultivation of subjects toward these ends. Prescription applies to the official mandatory regulations that bind and authorize the power of the enactment of statutory laws. Included in this is authorization to establish principles and standards, to develop learning and teaching formulas, and to draft rules of application and usage with methodology.

Didactic teaching is enlightened teaching and edifying instruction. It illuminates, directs, and guides the pupil through the learning process and coaches him through self-study and discovery. Didactics includes pedagogy. It is education that contains cultural enrichment, perceptive insight, and lectures with preaching and exhortative overtones. It includes homiletic disciplines and emphasizes the scholastic and academic precepts and principles of the subject of its knowledge. Pedagogy consists of the core studies needed to lay a foundation for future education, especially for areas of specialization. It stresses through its curriculum healthy social attitudes, life skills, and preparation useful for world knowledge and enriched living. Historical background, sociological foundations, and the like are therefore to be found in pedagogic teaching.

As you can see, the role of the teacher in the Body of Christ is vital. They are the reason the church will grow, expand, and enrich itself and others. A church without teaching is likely to stagnate, be stunted, remain immature, or fall into perverted or extreme forms of worship and service. A church who takes seriously the Great Commission will have an organized department for teaching its members. It will go to great lengths to identify and equip members to take on the teaching mandate Christ left. Some churches have whole institutions devoted to the education of not only its own members, but of the general Body as well. They turn out the most teachers, and can be strict about the quality of knowledge they receive and dispense. They are emphatic in their education standards for those who instruct in their schools.

What Is a Teacher?

A teacher is one who effectively imparts knowledge to others. Effectively means here, "results-getting" knowledge. Teachers in Christ's kingdom communicate truth, life, holiness, salvation, and sanctification to the Body. They may also prepare others to enter the ministry. The teaching responsibility is as great at its demands. The range of subjects Christian teachers can cover is basic Bible study to post graduate level studies, for those already in Christ's service. As you can see, the possibilities are endless. Teachers may also give students basic academic skills, instruct them on the life skills of the Kingdom, train them for professional occupations, or in many other ways equip them for a fruitful life of Christian service and discipleship.

Teachers mostly impart knowledge to others. But they also determine the knowledge needs of others and investigate ways of meeting those needs through the development and implementation of programs to address the needs in a formal or informal setting. Innovative teachers use all of God's creation as their classroom and seek to make their sessions invigorating, informative, enlightening, and interesting. They also know the importance and success of drawing the student into his own learning process and enabling him to help himself grasp the knowledge being presented to him. Therefore, their lessons will integrate a good amount of mandatory student involvement as a means of imparting knowledge to their students.

To best understand what this involves, a brief list of its high points is below to give you an idea of how a teacher thinks and what a teacher instinctively understands about helping people learn. To impart knowledge is to dispense the following:

I. Training and education

2. Study guidance and application tools

3. Skill development exercises and activities

4. Application/practice proficiency exercises

5. Discipline/correction and remediation drills

6. Maturation skills
7. Evaluation /appraisal criteria

8. Reinforcement, continuing education guidance

9. Utility knowledge examples

10. Productivity knowledge approaches

Assignment: Define and illustrate each one of the above for class discussion.

The above requires logical, orderly study habits and research skills, as well as wide-reaching, multi-dimensional vision. It takes evaluation ability so that only relevant, useful information is compiled and assimilated to give to the students. They are administered efficiently, expediently, and economically.

The teacher's ministry also calls for foresight and insight, strong intuitive ability, and critical thinking. This requirement considers:

- What learners need to know
- Why they need to know it
- How to best get knowledge across to them

- How they are to use knowledge once it is acquired

- What learners may expect from acquired knowledge
- The impact knowledge will have on their community or environment.
- How to best apply, cultivate, and strengthen their knowledge
- How their knowledge is to be regulated by discipline
- What makes knowledge valuable to the church
- How to determine when, where, and how knowledge is to be built on
- The most effective stages and degrees to administer knowledge
- The best methods of instruction

- How to plan, present, evaluate, correct and observe learning programs for the benefit of the student and the educating organization

The teaching anointing, once developed, thinks consistently along these lines.

Assignment: Pair off and develop, as a team, explanation outlines for the above to share with a group of students in their New Teacher Education Class.

Chapter Nine Review 2

1. What are the two main Scriptures used for teachers?

2 Name and define the four Greek terms used in the explanation.

3. Explain pedagogy and state its place in Christian education.

4. Give an example of pedagogy in course.

5. Summarize a teacher.

6. Review knowledge impartation.

7. State the 5 features teachers' skills call for.

8.   What 13 things constitute a teacher's normal considerations?

Essential Teaching Functions

1. Course development, lesson planning and preparation, curriculum development and execution are major responsibilities of this office.

2. Knowledge progression in respect to developing people, follow up, follow through, and reinforcement, as well as learning assessments and remediation are vital to the post. The skills and ability required to do this are great.

Instructor is to lecture the forms and modes to communicate these.

The Personality of the Office

l.   Teachers are basically hungry for knowledge and eager to learn what they readily perceive as beneficial to others. You will hardly catch a genuine teacher casual about knowledge. Even when his formal education is finished, the teacher will want to keep fresh by adding to his knowledge new information.

2.   Teachers have the capacity for taking in huge amounts of information, sifting and sorting through it, and utilizing it for their own growth and the growth of others. They innately understand what stunts or promotes scholastic growth and are dutiful about exploring ways to relieve it. Teachers are able to study for long periods of time and extract critical material from reading texts quite easily. They sense the relevance and usefulness of certain subject matter to their classes. They tend toward criticalness in respect to the accuracy of knowledge and the perfection of what they learn and have a strong demand for high quality output, as it is seen as a push to student effort, and thus an intangible contribution to overall development.

3.   Teachers understand why people avoid learning, and what makes it difficult for some of them to learn. Quickly they discern and identify typical hindrances to the learning process. This ability is enhanced by teachers' determination to strive to do something about it. Few teachers are comfortable with their students' being caught in a failure chain. Even less will be indifferent toward it, which is always to the detriment of their students.

4.   Teachers have an inclination toward research and investigation of facts. They usually do not like to give out misinformation, as they understand the difficulty the student will have replacing it with the accurate. Generally they don't like to "wing" it, either, and prefer to avoid standing up before their students unprepared or unenlightened.

5.   Teachers are structured, orderly thinkers who deliberate extensively over new information and constantly seek to upgrade the quality and content of the knowledge they possess for the material they teach. Their preparation is likely to include the most ingenious learning aids, as they study long on how to best educate their students on new or difficult material.

6.   Teachers are methodical and function best when they have been able to arrange what they teach, or put learning into some type of rational system. To them learning, whether or not

the student knows it, is a systematic process. Therefore, they are notorious for developing creative formulas to ease memorization and retention efforts and streamline study habits.

7.   Good teachers rely on creativity and innovation to help people learn. They also know the value of visual aids, field projects, and special learning activities to reduce the boredom that can dry up the learning atmosphere of their classes.

8.   Tenderness toward learning deficiencies and the problems that cause or intensify them is evidence of the dedicated teacher. They make students with special problems a personal mission and take pleasure in seeing those who struggled to achieve go on to excel. For a teacher, the functional and productive student is their greatest reward.

9.   A commitment to student progress and learning success in terms of right application of material taught is characteristic of the office.

10.   Teachers are critical thinkers, with a deep desire to solve the problems they encounter. They push to turn out problem solvers and critical thinkers themselves. They are also performance driven and can unavoidably fall into over use of evaluation systems and appraisal programs, which may be overbearing on weaker students. Teacher insight makes them typically good designers of such systems with reliable indicators of their student's potentials, strength, and weaknesses.

11.   Teachers possess the ability to follow, as well as execute and enhance, established curricula. A distinguishing trait found in those who are ordained teachers is their ability to understand and adhere to curriculum syllabuses while effectively varying them to suit the individual needs of their students. They do so without sacrificing quality or consistency.

12.   Teachers are generally intolerant of stagnation, and therefore quickly discard outdated information while shunning that which offers no tangible benefit to their students. Their judgment in this area, for true teachers, is peerless. They also enjoy attending meetings and conventions, if they are pertinent to their field, to expand their knowledge and update their methods and approaches. Freshness is key to a teacher's ability to diversify material, and while they enjoy novel ideas, teachers are put off by anything that destroys what they know to be sound principles of study and learning. Fundamentals are important to them, and foundations are highly valued.

13.   Teaching instincts rapidly decide on what works for students on the basis of the teacher's ability to sense the temperament, composition, and fundamental strengths and weaknesses of his or her class as a whole and the students severally. Usually they do not waste time with what will not work, knowing to do so is frustrating to the students and themselves.

14.   Teachers realize the need for basic controls, authority, and organization to a mission and usually respect procedures outlined by their administration. However, they are quick to express their need for flexibility and latitude and want administrators to include this need in their overall structure demands.

What the Office Demands

1. Diligence, intuition, insight, and empathy

2. Order, methodology, and procedural understanding

3. A cooperative, outgoing, flexible attitude toward the work
4. Strong organization, structure, leadership, and interactive skills

5. An understanding of the place and use of organized and creative learning programs and materials in their ministries
6. Good planning and implementation expertise
7. Excellent communication and listening skills
8. Commitment, conscientiousness, and faithfulness
9. Good people sensing and classroom sensing skills
10. A strong command of audience/student attention
11. Talent for student development and nurturing
12. Curriculum development and implementation
13. A knack for inspiring learning and growth
14. A gift for involving students in their learning
15. Ability to motivate attendance, performance, and completion

Exercise:
Use the 15 points above to design a screening survey and training guide for engaging ten new instructors in your school.

Chapter Nine Review 3

1.   Discuss numbers 1-4 in terms of recognizing and confirming teachers.

2.   Use 4-6 to evaluate a teacher's attitude and performance, and draft your own standards and guidelines for them.

3.   Numbers 7-11 make a good guide for developing a teacher training program. Give an extensive example of what yours would be like.

4.   Use 12-14 to show how you would remediate a troubled teacher on your staff.

APPENDICIES

Authority

Simply speaking, authority is **the lawful right to enforce obedience, to give orders, and to direct the behavior or conduct of others over whom one has charge.** Loosely stated, authority is synonymous with power; however, it is more accurate to say that *authority is established by* power; that is, applied force or the threat of it. Only in an environment where there exists the conference of power can authority be firmly established. Where there is no power, there can be no authority. Authority has no basis to exist, having no enforcement outlet to maintain and affect its ends.

Although authority is frequently abused, it is, nevertheless, still a necessary factor in leadership Otherwise there is no mechanism of influence and control to assure those who start. out with you in your mission or charge will put forth genuine and quality effort, and properly do their part in bringing the vision to pass on a consistent basis. Furthermore, authority and power are effective in dealing with those who would oppose or endanger a movement or deter other workers from their labors. Incidents of anarchy, rebellion, and resistance are redressed through the use of authority (See Proverbs 29:19 and 20:30).

Consider, for instance, in viewing the essential place of authority, the accounts of Ezra and Nehemiah who had both received charges from the Lord God of Israel to repair the temple and rebuild the wall of Jerusalem. In order for them to do so, being captives to another nation, they needed the authority to initiate the work, even to enlist the help of the people.

They derived their authority from the decree of Cyrus the king, who had the power to allow or disallow their actions. His authority included enforcement power so they could complete their task in the face of opposition, hostility, or revolt, which was actually the reason Cyrus was born and ascended to power. The authority, therefore, that Cyrus had was from God (See 2 Chronicles 36:22,23 and Ezra 1:2-8) and it was by his divinely appointed position he authorized the Jews to begin the work which God had commanded Cyrus to see to. If the king were not in agreement, the very attempt to rebuild God's house could have gotten them killed. In this case it was the other way around. Cyrus' decree meant that anyone who opposed the work could be killed. People unavoidably attack leadership to indirectly assault a venture or movement because advancing and building always seems like a threat to their convenience and complacency. Fear of change makes them worry about their comforts and pleasure. Building and progress mean change, and change can be scary and disruptive; so they resist it for these and other reasons. Knowing this quirk of humanity, Cyrus gave the edict which preserved their labors and the people who performed them.

Authority is critical because most people, when in groups, cannot agree or remain in harmony and unity for extended periods of time. Personal pursuits, preferences, and perspectives inevitably surface to divide and confuse them. Fear of being bossed or taken advantage of or abused makes them begin to doubt the validity of their association and lead them to contend with the leaders. It is a known fact that groups of people on their own accord cannot come into one mind on an issue and maintain that focused agreement for any length of time without a leader. Someone will have to keep their eyes pointed toward the goal, set the priorities for success, and keep victory ever before them. If not, when tedium, longevity, setbacks, and obstacles begin to take their toll, they will challenge the work and attempt to escape using any means they can. The possibility of this occurring increases greatly when groups have to value and prioritize more than one issue at once, or if they are to decide the most effective way of tackling a mass endeavor. All these reasons are likely to stress a group. The larger its number the greater the prospect of stressing its bond of cohesiveness, making the potential of their completing the job at hand without leadership less and less. Numerous other factors can contribute to the breach of unity that will cause the divisiveness responsible for the failure of the mission. Chief of them is the faultiness of basic human nature. Its frailties mean there has to be a focal point for them to look to for direction, problem resolution, and guidance on the way to their goal. Leaders have the temperament, restraint, discipline, and insight to provide at critical stages the focus followers need to get work done and to continue until success is seen.

Once the suitable person has been identified and appointed, a large part of the distracting factors previously hindering the work disappear. Their presence and skill see to that. However, such a person must be invested with the authority to do what it takes to benefit those who trust him to enforce the will of the majority on the few opposers. Trust, consequently, is a big part of leadership. The people must perceive that an atmosphere of safety, integrity, and ethics exists enough for them to relax their guards and defenses and establish. the unity achievement requires. The sense of safety and well-being must foster within them the belief that justice, equity, and balance will prevail with those whom they entrust their leadership to. Any delegation of authority, because of this, has to convey this to those who follow, else the entire structure is vulnerable. Authority, as we have said, implies power and both can negatively affect a group's support of its leaders. An element of force, furthermore, is needed to assure compliance, conformance, and performance demanded by the authority. This is known as the enforcement arm of authority. The enforcement arm naturally implies power. Without these there can be no motive for obedience, and as a result, little or no success. The vision is not achieved because the goal is not realized. Only the fruit of failure, disillusionment, and disappointment are witnessed. Followers are now bitter and cynical; leaders are now confused and insecure. Everyone walks away defeated due to the breakdown of authority. Authority, therefore, is native to leadership, and only in an environment where leaders are clearly established and respected can the only efficient means of getting a project complete take place.

Such was the case with Ezra and Nehemiah, and things haven't changed a bit since then. Even today the principle of authority and power are yet in place for the kingdoms established by God to operate on this very premise.

Authority, Law, and Order

God is law and order. Chaos, revolt, and rebellion did not originate with him. They originated with Lucifer, who in attempting to exalt himself above his Maker, instigated the first revolt to ever take place in creation. Until iniquity was found in him, the disruption of law and order in creation was not a problem (See Isaiah 14:9 and Ezekiel 23; 28:1-19).

Ministerial training, for this reason, must be predicated on the reality that law and order are the substance of the Lord's created worlds. It is through them He rules and reigns. The hook of Daniel confirms this when it says, "the Most High rules in the kingdom of men and sets over them who he will" (Daniel 4:17; 34-37). The first thing to accept is that God rules. If this were not true then words like power, strength, might, authority, force, and dominion would not be included in the language of God. They are included, however, and are written for our insight and wisdom.

In like manner, words like order, obedience, rule, and government would not be factors in God's revelation of himself and his leadership. There is government in all of the worlds he created, and there are those who have been created and thus ordained to rule under him or on his behalf:

It is interesting to note, in view of the divine establishment. of authority, few actually question God's right to rule. They may challenge His rule, or even His existence or sovereignty as Creator, but once the question of God as an eternal living being is settled, there is little doubt as to whether or not He has the power or authority to rule. The unfortunate thing, in respect to this, is that when people come into the realm of God, the church, they expect law and order to prevail without human leaders. Somehow they think God will inspirationally and invisibly do what has been done by humans in the secular world within the church world, without their having to respect and obey appointed Christian leaders. The Lord, in giving the earth over into the hands of sons of men, ordained law and order be enforced by Him through those He appointed as leaders. Even though it is true the chief ruler over all things is God, his indirect leadership is ordained through man.

Think of God's kingdom as one vast conglomerate with thousands of departments and subordinates assigned to staff, manage, and govern. Who would have a problem with the idea of his or her company's having a staff, supervisor, manager, vice president, president, and so forth? If you took the conglomerate example a little further, expanding it to reflect not only departments but subsidiaries, corporations, companies, and so on, the establishment of leaders to manage and govern the different branches within the entities would still be understood; yet because God is actually the possessor and head over all and the Church, the Church struggles with his order within it. At the same time, the Body understands and even esteems secular organizational principles because it is perceived to be of man. Nevertheless, Colossians 1:15-18 and Ephesians 1:20-22 say God, that is the Godhead, is over all things. Peter tells us angels, principalities, and powers are subject to Him. So, God rules.

God rules because he is God. He derived his authority from having existed before anything ever was. He tells us in his word that he is the Alpha and Omega; First and Last; Beginning and Ending. God is the reason all things exist and the cause of all that takes place in creation. Before Him nothing existed. He is why everything we see today is. Because of this God rules. People, on the other hand, rule or lead because God ordained it so. One of many biblical examples of this is Cyrus, the king we discussed in the last section, in the book of Isaiah. The Bible says in many places how and why people are placed in their leadership positions. Don't conclude this only applies to church leaders, a mistake made by believers and unbelievers alike. It applies to *all things*. God is God in all His creation, and He has given this authority into the hands of His Son, Jesus Christ. As far as people are concerned, God instilled within them at creation the capacity to lead and rule. The problem is that when He did so, his intent was, ideally, that they would do so according to His way—although He knew they eventually would not. However, the original plan was that man, who was created in the image and likeness of God, would rule like his God, and not like one of His lesser creatures.

Nevertheless, all things having been made and completed before the foundation of the world, the calls and ordinations remained unchanged. Whatever the Lord ordained His creatures were born to do, they would do the same. Leadership and obedience breakdowns seen are the product of sin's dominion, observed today in godly or ungodly leadership. God, regardless, expects godly leading from those who are His born again children, those filled with his Spirit (godly being that which exemplifies and upholds His kingdom, its righteousness, morals, and standard of life). All this is to say that God ordained Christian leaders, as well as world leaders, to do their jobs in accordance with His Word. In the Church, every flock is to have leaders: a shepherd, a prophet, teacher, and evangelist. Most would spring from the initiatives, expansions, and maintenance of an apostle. Shepherdless flocks are contrary to Scripture. Our Judges example showed why God cannot endorse this: His people invariably wander from the truth and begin to do things their own way. They embrace pagan ways and integrate sin into their doctrines and culture. Throughout Scripture, there is not one instance where God left sheep without a shepherd. Nor is it found in His Word where sheep instruct or are to lead their shepherds. The unstable vein of human nature, because of these factors, makes Christian leadership essential.

Christian leadership exists because God ordained it, for the same reasons all the other powers that be were ordained. Recognizing people's proneness to stray, wander, fall into sin, and become resistant to God, and therefore distort his Word to obscure and pervert the truth, God installed at creation leaders people could identify with and relate to naturally over spiritually. Furthermore, residual Adamic lingerings which cause people to fight and abuse each other and become inflated with foolish pride meant restraining mechanisms would be needed within man's cultures for the protection of societies. Meanwhile, for others who occupy themselves with the world, failing to read and study the very Scriptures that give them life, leaders are given to exhort and guide; subsequently, preventing them from shutting themselves out of the blessings of their covenant and exposing themselves instead to the Lord's chastening and judgments. Lastly, God's people will be vulnerable to Satanic seductions and demonic onslaught, which they are unequipped to defend against, without sound, potent leadership. The total consequence of these is chaos, confusion, suffering, lack, and delusion, which will invade a body deprived of a head. All problems leaders—all leaders—were made to resolve. Leaderless entities firmly entrench the doctrine of unbelief most devastating to the church, weakening its godly moorings. The church then forsakes its stance of holiness and mainstreams itself into the institutionalized cultures of society, no longer able to tell the differences between the persuasions of the two, to the detriment of the kingdom of God. Its loss of discernment and sanctification is what gives rise to the Prophetic Mantle crucial to contemporary society. Prophets are the ones who champion the call to repent and return to the true and living God. They thus restore order to the church and clarity of thought to its teachings. Their efforts, like that which was spearheaded by the prophecies of Huldah the Prophetess under Josiah's regime, sway the balance of power back into the hands of God and return hope to the people of their time.

Orders and Authorities: Powers, Positions, Levels and Dimensions of Anointings

To best understand the material to come, you'll need to know how the Lord organized and governs the kingdoms he created from the beginning. The Scriptures that best support our discussion are Romans 13:1-8 and 1 Peter 2:13-14. Romans reads,

"Let every soul be subject to the governing authorities. For there is no authority except from God, and the authorities (powers) that exist (be) are appointed by God. Therefore, whoever resists the authority resists the ordinance of God, and these who resist will bring judgment on themselves. For rulers are not a terror to good works but to evil. Do you want to be unafraid of the authority? Do what is good, and you will have praise from the same. For he is God's minister to you for good. But if you do evil, be afraid; for he does not hear the sword in vain; for he is God's minister, an avenger to execute wrath on him who practices evil. Therefore, you must be subject, not only because of wrath but also for conscience sake." (Romans 13:1-5, NKJV)

Matthew 22:21 and Acts 5:35-39 together explain what our Romans passage of Scripture is talking about. Acts, in support, shows the dangers of fighting against God's ordained authorities. 1 Peter 2:13-14 further admonishes us on this subject:

"Therefore submit yourselves to every ordinance of man for the Lord's sake, whether to the king as supreme, or to governors, as to those who are sent by him for the punishment of evildoers and for the praise of those who do good." (NKJV)

What the four references have in common is the depiction of God's ordained institutions. Authority is an outgrowth of them; however, our discussions are centering on the authorities themselves, and their place in the ministry of the prophet. The charts following this discussion enlarge the Scripture depictions, and give us a global look at the ordained orders and authorities of God.

God's Layers of Power

The purpose of this information is simple and may be stated in just one brief sentence: *A leader cannot come into his or her power without first receiving the fullness of knowledge and understanding related to it!* Needless to say, the beginning and head of all powers and all that we will yet be discussing is God: literally, the **Godhead**—God the Father, God the Son, and God the Holy Spirit. They are spirit and make up the substance, according to Hebrews 11, of all power in both the spiritual and the natural realms. "Substance," for your edification, means stuff, body, or corporal structure. In the physical realm, it applies to the touch, feel, taste, smell, see, and hear world we live in. In the spirit they define the basic nature, principle, drive, energy, and impulse of all we naturally see, touch, taste, smell, and hear.

The third level of power and authority is **man**. He constitutes the reflective shadow of he spiritual forces that give him drive, shape, and energy. Above man and beneath the Godhead is the second strata of the power structure instituted by God, and that is the **angels**. They make up the subordinate layer of spiritual power that links level three with level one. So, spiritual power is motivated and exercised by the Godhead, animated by the angels, and exerted by humans (See Colossians 1:15-18; 1 Peter 3:21,22; Hebrews 1:1-14; John 17:15; Isaiah 44:6-8; 24-26).

Scriptures relating to and/or supporting the above may be seen below:

Text	Explanation
1. John 1:51	Angels serving the Son of Man
2. Genesis 28:12	Angels serving Jacob
3. Acts 5:19	Angels with power to overturn the civil laws that arrested the apostles
4. Acts 27 :23	Angela keeping Paul in the midst of a crisis and assuring him of the certain fulfillment of the word of the Lord

Class of Authority

Why does authority exist? According to our passages, it exists for the following reasons:

1. Terrorize evil

2. Praise good

3. Act as God's temporal minister

4. Punish evil

5. Execute the wrath of God on injustice and ungodliness

6. Receive taxes to finance its institutions

7. Administrate temporal affairs of the earth

They exist within every strata of God's creation and apply to every class of his creatures. Classes of authority as ordained by God are listed below:

CLASS	MEANING
Thrones	Regional reigns governing cultural beliefs, trends, and movements that inspire a nation, country, or its societies.
Dominion	Field of endeavors and range of expertise in professions that dominate the occupational provinces of a people and their land's empires.

Principality	The territory of a reigning prince; a prince's jurisdiction; sovereignty under a king or monarch.
Powers	Restraining or dominating influence expressed in might, force, and strength. Authority to act, engage in power-related actions; to instigate and initiate power-related activities. The innate or intrinsic capacity or ability to exercise or apply the aforementioned.
Rulers	Those authorized to govern, regulate, and control a populace; to supervise and administrate the affairs of a country, sphere, or domain.
Kingdom	The province or territory of a king in which a regent has unbridled authority and dominion to exercise or exert power and authority as he sees fit.
Authorities	Institutions formed for the organized dispensation of power. The influence, government, enforcement, and control of something or someone.

NOTE: *Power is demonstrated when enforcement and control are needed.*

Chart One

Layers Two & Three
RULERS
CHRIST
KING OF KINGS

Angels—*Spirit*	Humans—*Natural*
gods- Sovereign spherical authority	gods- Sovereign responsibility
lords- Dominion	lords- Dominion
Princes	Princes- Under rule authority
King- Supreme	King- Supreme
Authorities- Governors	Authorities- Governors
Rulers- Guardians	Rulers- Guardians
Powers- Judicature	Powers- Judicature
Ministers- Enforcers/executioners	Ministers- Enforcers/executioners

Scriptures relating to and/or supporting the above:

Text	**Explanation**
Jeremiah 48:1	Nebo is Babylon's god of science and literature
Jeremiah 49:1-6	Milcom is the Ammonite god *Molech*
Ezekiel 28:1-10	Human king
Ezekiel 28: 12-19	Spiritual king

There are spiritual forces occupying the same positions in the heavenlies that humans occupy in the earth. The distinction is the actions and decisions of the spirit realm always precede and determine those of the natural. This applies to the angelic and the demonic kingdoms. The time lag between the initiatives of the spirit and the response of the natural can be years or centuries apart.

Chart Two

Layers 2 & 3

KINGDOMS

Angels—*Spiritual*	Humans—*Natural*
Thrones- Kingdom	Throne- Kingdom
Principality- Prince's realm	Principality- Prince's realm
Jurisdiction- Center of domination	Jurisdiction- Center of domination
Dominion- Heavenly stronghold	Dominion- stronghold
Sphere- Strata of power and authority	Sphere- Strata of power and authority
Territories- Supernatural zones	Territories- Geographic zones
Regions- Realms of operational influence	Regions- lands of operational influence
Districts- Sector of guardianship	Districts- Sector of guardianship
Nations- Tongues and races	Nations- Countries

Scriptures relating to and/or supporting the above:

Text	Explanation
1 Chronicles 21	David's unrighteous census inspired by demonic forces.
2 Samuel 24:15-17	Angels used to execute the wrath of God

Just as there are natural forces assigned areas over which they govern and wield influence, the supernatural world is the same. Tracking with what we know to exist in the natural, supernatural forces engineer and instigate what takes place in the world.

Chart Three

Layers 2 & 3

POWER COMPARISON

ANGELS	*CHURCH*
Feeds into the Church	Feeds into the Bodies
Principality (rules)	Principality (influence)
Dominion (controls)	Dominion (intervenes)
Jurisdiction (realm to exercise authority)	Judicature (altars decisions through prayer)
Regions (areas on the earth)	Spheres (cultural impact of church)
Countries (where angels control)	Communities (where church is placed)
Populations (ethnic sphere of influence)	Societies (cultural impact of church)
Church (bodies of religions)	Congregations (where church is placed)
Persons (carnal/temporal life)	Souls (eternal existence)

God's Ordained Distributions

Governors (rulers)	Government (Admin./exec. control)
Powers- Supernatural	Powers- Dynamic
spiration (motivate)	Influence (affect)
Watchers (observe, guard, protect)	Watchmen (observe, guard, defend)
Judicative (effecting judgment)	Judgment (declare, dispense, convict)
Enlighten- (expose)	Enforce (admonish, uphold, defend)
Execute (heavenly commands)	Intercede (pray, supplicate, war)

As you can see, the two layers overlap but are distinct in their effect. Again, the spiritual impresses and manipulates the natural (See 1 Kings 22:19-23; Judges 9:23; Joshua 5:13-15. Refer also to Exodus 23:20-27).

Manifestation of the Holy Spirit of God

Word of Wisdom	Word of Knowledge
Faith	Gifts of Healings
Working of Miracles	Prophecy
Discerning of Spirits	Diverse Tongues
Interpretation of Tongues	

In the space below, write your present understanding of the basic difference between a manifestation and a gift. Explain the significance of the difference to both, the Church at large, and the ministry.

GIFTS

General Classification

NATIVE GIFTS OF THE SPIRIT

ROMANS 12

Prophecy	Faith
Ministry	Teaching
Exhortation	Liberality
Leadership	Mercy
Stewardship	Oration
Revelation	Activities

As you can easily see, these are quite different from the previous list since they are not the same as the 1 Corinthians manifestations. Comment on what you see as the distinct differences in the space below. Conclude with the application differences between the two, both in ministry and in the believer's life.

God's Gifts Of Grace

Here is a list of the Gifts of Grace dispensed to mankind for the eventual or ultimate work of the ministry and their explanations. They are biblically based.

Romans 12:6-8:

Faith	Unwavering belief in God and his Word, even in the face of severe trials; those who can just believe for belief's sake.
Prophecy	Inspired utterances received spontaneously from the supernatural, but generally accurate predictions.
Ministry	Special motivation to devote one's life to the service of God and his Church, as well as humanity.
Teaching	Extraordinary ability to impart and comprehend the most effective means of administering knowledge and imparting it to learners.
Exhortation	The gift of persuasive, provocative preaching encompassing admonishments, entreaties, and counsel that spurs listeners to persistent obedience in action.
Liberality	Generosity in service, commitment, and giving; philanthropy.
Leadership	High ability to direct, manage, and govern persons and resources efficiently to complete a vision's mission.

Mercy	Intense motivation to render sacrificial relief services, physical aid, and similar assistance to the suffering, distressed, and disadvantaged.

Peter 4:10,11:

Stewardship	The propensity for diligent and efficient oversight of another's affairs.
Oration	A special talent for effective verbal communications.

1 Corinthians 12:1-4

Ministries	A remarkable comprehension of the particulars of service, and an interpretation of how they are to be arranged for the advancement of a cause, mission, and people.
Activities	Designated divisions of charges, duties, and responsibilities required by leadership for support and success.

Ephesians 3:1-5

Revelation	Incisive apprehension of supernatural disclosures, and a penchant for receiving them more than others.

CPSIA information can be obtained
at www.ICGtesting.com
Printed in the USA
BVHW010927020320
573813BV00004B/183